# CHURCH LAW & TAX REPORT

# *The 1998 Compensation Handbook for Church Staff*

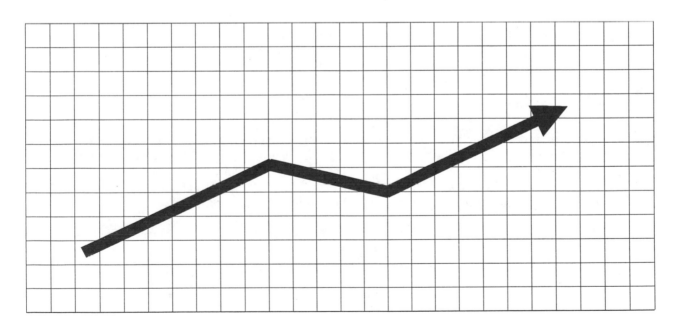

James F. Cobble, Jr., D.Min., Ed.D. & Richard R. Hammar, J.D., LL.M., CPA

Christian Ministry Resources
PO Box 1098
Matthews, NC 28106
(704) 841-8066
Fax (704) 841-8039

# Table of contents

93/03

# Chapter 1

# *Introduction*

Welcome to *The 1998 Compensation Handbook for Church Staff*. Please take a few minutes to read this introduction. It provides several ways to maximize your use of this book.

The *Compensation Handbook* was developed to provide church leaders and employees with a current and reliable picture of compensation practices across a broad spectrum of American churches. It presents survey data from over 2,000 churches representing more than 9,000 staff members. The survey data was obtained between January, 1997 and April, 1997 from churches that subscribe to *Church Law & Tax Report, Church Treasurer Alert!,* or *Church Secretary's Communique*. This information can play an important role in determining equitable compensation packages for church staff members. The *Compensation Handbook* can help you:

- to determine appropriate compensation levels for nine key pastoral, professional, and support staff positions.

- to develop effective compensation packages—guidelines are given to maximize net income while remaining in compliance with federal tax laws.

- to provide church workers with a statistical framework for evaluating their present compensation package—comparisons can be made regarding church size, budget, setting, and other important variables.

- to develop an objective standard for evaluating requests for raises and changes in benefits.

- to assist denominational offices and other ecclesiastical organizations in promoting equitable and fair compensation practices within their churches.

- to better understand the nature of church compensation planning.

## How To Make The Best Use Of This Book

Anyone engaged in compensation planning for church staff members should first become familiar with some basic federal tax laws. How a compensation package is structured can either help or hurt a church staff member. Chapter 2 provides a detailed discussion of the major tax laws that affect the compensation of church staff, and provides tax saving tips.

Chapter 3 provides guidance on reading and using the data found in the tables throughout this book. Included is an example that illustrates how to determine compensation ranges for a senior pastor. The same process can be used for all staff positions.

Chapter 4 provides comparisons between the national averages of the nine staff positions included in this study. The chapter begins by providing an employment profile for each staff position. Table 4-3 provides a comparative ranking of each position along with the standard deviation for each national average. Standard deviation is an important statistical calculation that is explained in both chapters 3 and 4. Denominational comparisons are also presented in this chapter.

Chapters 5-13 provide detailed information on each individual staff position. Natural curiosity will pull most church staff members immediately to the chapter which presents data about their position. Remember, though, understanding chapters 2 and 3 is critical to using this book in an effective manner.

Finally, chapter 14 provides a statistical abstract of the churches participating in this study.

# Data Analysis

Inconclusive or faulty survey data were not included in the survey. Figures that appeared unrealistic or way outside the normal distribution were eliminated to avoid skewing the results. These results represent the churches that participated in the survey. The sampling population used was a fair representation of American churches, but certain church sizes, budget sizes, and denominations have a stronger representation than others. To the extent possible, we have attempted to organize the data in ways that avoid small samples. At times, however, small samples simply reflect a reality such as rural churches with an attendance over 1,000, or churches smaller than 100 with a full-time business administrator. Nevertheless, sample size should be taken into account when considering the value of any particular finding. Standard deviations were calculated for the average compensation of each position. Some variables, however, reflected more of a linear relationship with compensation than did others. That relationship also changed from one position to another. The Pearson product-moment correlation coefficient was calculated to determine the strength of relationship between compensation and church size, and compensation and church budget for each of the nine positions. Coefficients of determination and nondetermination were also calculated to gain a better intuitive notion of the strength of the relationships between size and compensation, and budget and compensation. While this study does not make explicit reference to those findings, they do provide the basis for the inferences made at various points within the text about correlations.

Finally, we have endeavored to make this book both useful and easy to use. Your feedback on how to improve is indeed welcome.

# Chapter 2

# *Compensation Planning*

*Synopsis. Compensation planning for clergy and other church staff presents several unique issues that are not well understood by many church leaders and their advisers. This chapter clears away the confusion and presents 19 key considerations to review while doing compensation planning.*

Most churches will adopt 1998 compensation packages for their clergy and church staff in the final months of 1997. Now is a good time to review several possible components of a compensation package. Consider the following.

**1. Salary.** The most basic component of church staff compensation is salary. There are two important considerations to keep in mind with respect to staff salaries—the amount of the salary, and the use of "salary reduction agreements." These two issues will be discussed separately.

**a. Amount**. Staff salaries ordinarily are set by the church board. Churches generally may pay any amount they wish, with one very big exception—if a church pays unreasonably high compensation to a pastor or other employee there are two possible consequences:

*(1) Loss of tax-exempt status.* In order for a church or any other charity to maintain its tax-exempt status, it must meet a number of conditions. One condition is a prohibition on the payment of unreasonably high compensation to any person. There are two considerations to note. First, very few charities have lost their exempt status for paying unreasonable compensation. The IRS has been very reluctant to impose this remedy. Few if any legitimate churches have lost their exempt status on this ground. Second, the law does not define what amount of compensation is unreasonable, and neither the IRS nor the courts have provided much clarification. One federal appeals court concluded that combined annual income of $115,680 paid by a religious organization to its founder and his wife was *not* excessive. The court in the "PTL" bankruptcy case concluded that maximum reasonable compensation for Jim Bakker would have been $133,100 in 1984, $146,410 in 1985, $161,051 in 1986, and $177,156 in 1987. The court based its conclusions on a comparison of the salaries of other nonprofit officers in the state.

*(2) Intermediate sanctions.* In 1996 Congress enacted legislation targeting unreasonable compensation paid by charities, including churches. The new legislation permits the IRS to impose tough new "intermediate sanctions" on persons who are paid "excess benefits" (defined as unreasonable compensation). The IRS had asked Congress to authorize such sanctions as an alternative to revoking a charity's tax-exempt status. It is very important for church leaders to be familiar with the new intermediate sanctions, since they permit the IRS to assess large penalties against both

highly compensated persons and members of a governing board who authorized the excessive compensation. The intermediate sanctions the IRS can impose include the following:

• *Tax on disqualified persons.* A "disqualified person" (someone, like a senior pastor, with significant administrative responsibilities) who benefits from an excess benefit transaction is subject to an excise tax equal to 25 percent of the amount of the "excess benefit" (the amount by which actual compensation exceeds the fair market value of services rendered). This tax is paid by the disqualified person directly, not his or her employer.

• *Additional tax on disqualified persons.* If a disqualified person fails to "correct" the excess benefit by the time the IRS assesses the 25 percent tax, then the IRS can assess an additional tax of 200 percent of the excess benefit. The new law specifies that a disqualified person can "correct" the excess benefit transaction by "undoing the excess benefit to the extent possible, and taking any additional measures necessary to place the organization in a financial position not worse than that in which it would be if the disqualified person were dealing under the highest fiduciary standards."

• *Tax on organization managers.* If the IRS assesses the 25 percent tax against a disqualified person, it is permitted by the new law to impose an additional 10 percent tax on any "organization manager" (any officer, director, or trustee) who participates in an excess benefit transaction knowing it is such a transaction, unless the manager's participation "is not willful and is due to reasonable cause."

⊃ **Key point.** The new intermediate sanctions impose a substantial excise tax on members of a church's governing board who vote for a compensation package that the IRS determines to be unreasonable. This makes it essential for board members to carefully review the reasonableness of compensation packages.

⊃ **Key point.** The new law specifies that any transaction in which the amount of an economic benefit provided to a disqualified person is based on the revenues of the organization may result in unreasonable compensation. Congress instructed the IRS to draft regulations clarifying when such arrangements will be deemed to result in unreasonable compensation.

⊃ **Key point.** A committee report clarifies that charities, disqualified persons, and governing boards may rely on a "presumption of reasonableness" with respect to a compensation arrangement if it was approved by a board of directors (or committee of the board) that: (1) was composed entirely of individuals unrelated to and not subject to the control of the disqualified person involved in the arrangement; (2) obtained and relied upon objective "comparability" information, such as (a) compensation paid by similar organizations, both taxable and tax-exempt, for comparable positions, (b) independent compensation surveys by nationally recognized independent firms, or (c) actual written offers from similar institutions competing for the services of the disqualified person; and (3) adequately documented the basis for its decision.

⊃ **Key point.** The new law creates a presumption that a minister's compensation package is reasonable if approved by the church board who relied upon objective "comparability" information, including independent compensation surveys by nationally recognized independent firms. The most comprehensive compensation survey for church workers is this text. There is no doubt that the IRS will be placing heavy reliance on the data in this text in any attempt to impose intermediate sanctions against a minister.

⊃ **Key point.** The new intermediate sanctions apply to unreasonable compensation paid on or after September 14, 1995.

⊃ **Recommendation.** Churches that pay a minister (or any staff member) more than $100,000 in total annual compensation and fringe benefits should obtain a legal opinion from an experienced tax attorney confirming that the amount paid is not "unreasonable" and will not expose the employee or the board to intermediate sanctions.

✎ **Tax savings tip.** Ministers and other church staff members should carefully review their W-2 or 1099 to be sure that it does not report more income than was actually received. If an error was made, the church should issue a corrected tax form.

**b. Salary reduction agreements.** Many churches have established "salary reduction agreements" to handle certain staff expenses. The objective is to reduce a worker's taxable income, since only the income remaining after the various "reductions" is reported on the worker's W-2 or 1099 form at the end of the year. It is important for churches to understand that they cannot reduce a worker's taxable income through salary reductions *unless specifically allowed by law*.

Here are three ways that taxable income can be reduced through salary reduction agreements:

(1) *Tax-sheltered annuity contributions*. Salary reduction agreements can be used to contribute to a minister's tax-sheltered annuity (sometimes called a "403(b) annuity), so long as the salary reductions meet certain conditions.

(2) *"Cafeteria plans."* Salary reduction agreements also can be used to fund "cafeteria plans" (including "flexible spending arrangements") if several conditions are met. A cafeteria plan is a written plan established by an employer that allows employees to choose between cash and a "menu" of nontaxable benefits specified by law (including employer-provided medical insurance premiums, group-term life insurance, and dependent care).

(3) *Housing allowances*. As noted more fully below, a church can designate a portion of a minister's salary as a housing allowance, and the amount so designated is not subject to income tax if certain conditions are met.

⊃ **Observation.** In most cases, "salary reductions" will not accomplish the goal of reducing a minister's taxable income. The IRS released a regulation in 1991 prohibiting the widespread practice of funding "accountable" reimbursement arrangements through salary reductions. This topic is addressed later in this chapter.

**2. Housing allowance.** The most important tax benefit available to clergy who own or rent their homes is the housing allowance exclusion. Federal tax law permits a minister who owns or rents a home to exclude from gross income that portion of his or her compensation that is designated in advance as a "housing allowance" by the church or church board, and that is actually spent on housing expenses. A housing allowance exclusion for clergy who own their homes may not exceed the fair rental value of their home (furnished, including utilities). Unfortunately, many churches fail to designate a portion of a minister's compensation as a housing allowance, and thereby deprive ministers of an important tax benefit.

Ministers who live in a church-owned parsonage are permitted to exclude from their gross income the fair rental value of the parsonage. However, if they incur any out-of-pocket expenses in living in the parsonage (utilities, furnishings, repairs, etc.), such expenses may be excluded from gross income to the extent that they do not exceed that portion of their compensation designated in advance as a "parsonage allowance" by their employing church.

> ✎ **Tax savings tip.** Clergy who live in church parsonages, and who incur any out-of-pocket expenses in maintaining the parsonage (such as utilities, property taxes, insurance, furnishings, or lawn care), should be sure that their employing church designates in advance a portion of their annual compensation as a "parsonage allowance". The amount so designated is not included on the minister's W-2 or 1099 at the end of the year, to the extent that the minister in fact has expenses of at least that amount. This is a very important tax benefit for clergy living in church-provided parsonages. Unfortunately, many of these clergy are not aware of this benefit, or are not taking advantage of it.

Note that these exclusions are for federal income tax purposes only. Ministers cannot exclude the fair rental value of a parsonage or a housing allowance when computing their social security taxes.

> ⊃ **Recommendation.** Clergy should be sure that the designation of a 1998 housing or parsonage allowance is on the agenda of the church board for one of its final meetings in 1997. The designation should be an official action of the board or congregation, and it should be duly recorded in the minutes of the meeting. The IRS also recognizes designations included in employment contracts and budget line items—assuming in each case that the designation was duly adopted by the church board (or the congregation in a business meeting).

How much should a church board designate as a housing allowance? Many churches base the allowance on their minister's estimate of actual housing expenses for the new year. The church provides the minister with a form on which anticipated housing expenses for the new year are reported. For clergy who own their homes, the form asks for projected expenses in the following categories: down payment, mortgage payments, property taxes, property insurance, utilities, furnishings and appliances, repairs and improvements, maintenance, and miscellaneous. Many churches designate an allowance in excess of the anticipated expenses itemized by the minister. Basing the allowance solely on a minister's actual expenses will penalize the minister if housing expenses in fact turn out to be higher than expected. In other words, the allowance should take into account unexpected housing costs or inaccurate projections of expenses.

⊃ **Recommendation.** Plan a mid-year review of the housing allowance to make sure that the designated amount is sufficient to cover actual expenses.

⊃ **Observation.** The compensation survey summarized over the next several chapters reveals that housing allowances are claimed by several associate clergy, administrators, music directors, secretaries, and custodians. However, it is important to note that the housing allowance is available only if two conditions are met: (1) the recipient is a minister, and (2) the allowance is provided as compensation for services performed in the exercise of ministry. In many cases, these conditions will not be satisfied by associate clergy, administrators, music directors, secretaries, and custodians. See chapter 3 of Richard Hammar's *Church and Clergy Tax Guide* (available from the publisher of this text) for more information.

**3. Equity allowances.** Ministers who live in church-owned parsonages are denied one very important benefit of home ownership—the opportunity to accumulate "equity" in a home over the course of many years. Many ministers who have lived in parsonages during much of their active ministry often face retirement without housing. Their fellow ministers who purchased a home early in their ministry often can look forward to retirement with a home that is either substantially or completely debt-free. To avoid the potential hardship often suffered by a minister who lives in a parsonage, some churches increase their minister's compensation by an amount sometimes referred to as an "equity allowance"—the idea being to provide the minister with the equivalent of equity in a home. This is an excellent idea that should be considered by any church having one or more ministers living in church-provided housing. Of course, for the concept to work properly, the equity allowance should not be accessible by the minister until retirement. Therefore, some churches choose to place the allowance directly in a minister's tax-sheltered retirement account.

⊃ **Recommendation.** Equity allowances should also be considered by a church whose minister rents a home.

**4. Accountable business expense reimbursement policy.** One of the most important components of church staff compensation packages is an "accountable" business expense reimbursement arrangement. This benefit is available to both clergy and lay staff members alike. Under such an arrangement a church (1) reimburses only those business expenses that are properly substantiated within a reasonable time as to date, amount, place, and business purpose, and (2) requires any excess reimbursements (in excess of substantiated expenses) to be returned to the church. Churches should seriously consider adopting an accountable reimbursement policy for reimbursing staff business expenses. Such a policy has the following advantages:

☐ Church staff report their business expenses to the church rather than to the IRS.

☐ Church staff who report their income taxes as employees, or who report as self-employed and who are reclassified as employees by the IRS in an audit, avoid the limitations on the deductibility of employee business expenses. These include (1) the elimination of any deduction if the worker cannot itemize deductions on Schedule A (most taxpayers cannot), and (2) the deductibility of business expenses on Schedule A as an itemized expense only to the extent that these expenses exceed 2% of the worker's adjusted gross income.

☐　The so-called *Deason* allocation rule is avoided. Under this rule, clergy must reduce their business expense deduction by the percentage of their total compensation that consists of a tax-exempt housing allowance.

☐　The "50% limitation" that applies to the deductibility of business meals and entertainment expenses is avoided. Unless these expenses are reimbursed by an employer under an accountable plan, only 50% of them are deductible by either employees or self-employed workers.

☐　Church staff who report their income taxes as self-employed avoid the shock of being reclassified as an employee by the IRS in an audit and being assessed additional taxes.

⊃ **Observation.** Many clergy and other church staff members who report their income taxes as self-employed have been reclassified as employees by the IRS. The effect of this is to move their business expenses from Schedule C (where they are fully deductible), to Schedule A. The disadvantage of reporting these expenses on Schedule A is that most taxpayers do not have sufficient itemized deductions to use Schedule A—meaning that the deduction of business expenses is lost completely. And, even if a minister or other church staff member is able to use Schedule A, the business expenses can be deducted only to the extent that they exceed 2% of adjusted gross income.

⊃ **Observation.** The compensation survey summarized over the next several chapters reveals that many churches provide automobile allowances to their clergy and lay staff. In many cases, a church will simply provide a fixed dollar amount every month to a worker (for example, $300), and require no substantiation of business miles or any return of the amount by which the allowances exceed substantiated business expenses. Such a common arrangement is referred to as a "nonaccountable" reimbursement arrangement. The tax effect—all of the allowances must be added to the worker's W-2 or 1099 at the end of the year, and the worker can claim a business deduction on Schedule A (if an employee) or on Schedule C (if self-employed). If a worker is an employee with insufficient itemized deductions to use Schedule A, there is no deduction available for business expenses even though all of the full amount of the monthly allowances are added to taxable income. This is a very unfortunate tax result that can be avoided completely through an accountable reimbursement arrangement. For a sample board resolution adopting an accountable business expense reimbursement arrangement, see chapter 7 of Richard Hammar's *Church and Clergy Tax Guide*.

As noted above, the IRS released a regulation in 1991 prohibiting the widespread practice of funding accountable reimbursement arrangements through salary reductions. This regulation ended a common church practice that allowed many clergy to enjoy the advantages of an accountable plan without any additional cost to the church.

☞ **Example.** Assume that First Church pays Rev. G $500 each week, and also agrees to reimburse his substantiated business expenses for each month out of the first weekly payroll check for the following month. Assume further that Rev. G substantiated $300 of business expenses for January. The church issued Rev. G his customary check of $500 for the first week of February, but only $200 of this check represents taxable salary while the remaining $300 represents a nontaxable reimbursement under an accountable plan. Only the $200 salary component of this check is included on Rev. G's W-2 (or 1099) form at the end of the year. This arrangement was once common, and still is practiced by some churches. The 1991 IRS regulation does not prohibit the funding of business expense reimbursements out of salary reductions. Rather, a church's reimbursements under such arrangements cannot be "accountable."

⊃ **Key point.** The IRS ruled in 1993 that a regulation prohibiting the funding of business expense reimbursements under accountable plans may not be avoided by "salary restructuring" agreements.

**5. Travel expenses of a spouse.** A church should decide if it will be paying for any of the travel expenses of a spouse accompanying a minister or other staff member on a business trip. Reimbursing these expenses represents a significant benefit. Unfortunately, there is considerable confusion regarding the correct reporting of such reimbursements for tax purposes. If the spouse's presence on the trip serves a legitimate business purpose, and the spouse's travel expenses are reimbursed by the church under an accountable arrangement (described above) then the reimbursements represent a nontaxable fringe benefit. If these two requirements are not met, the reimbursements represent taxable income to the minister or other staff member.

▲ **Caution.** If either of these conditions is not met, then a church's reimbursement of a nonemployee spouse's travel expenses will represent taxable income to the minister or other staff member. The same applies to children who accompany a minister or staff member on a business trip.

**6. Church-owned vehicles.** Churches should consider the advantages of acquiring an automobile for staff members' church-related travel. Here's why. If a church purchases a car, and the church board adopts a resolution restricting use of the car to church-related activities, then the worker reports no income or deductions, and better yet, there are no accountings, reimbursements, allowances, or recordkeeping requirements. This assumes that the car is in fact used exclusively for church-related purposes, and the strict conditions specified in the income tax regulations are satisfied.

Commuting is always considered to be personal use of a car, and accordingly this procedure would not be available if a church allowed a worker to commute to work in a church-owned vehicle. Fortunately, the income tax regulations permit certain church employees who use a church-owned vehicle exclusively for business purposes except for commuting to receive all of the benefits associated with business use of a church-owned vehicle, if certain additional conditions are met.

Unfortunately, most churches that provide a staff member with a car do not consider either of these alternatives. Rather, they simply transfer the car to the individual and impose no limitations on personal use. This arrangement results in taxable income to the staff member, whether the staff member is a minister or a lay employee.

⊃ **Key point.** See chapter 4 of Richard Hammar's *Church and Clergy Tax Guide* for a full discussion of these rules.

**7. Self-employment tax.** Social security benefits are financed through two tax systems. Employers and employees each pay the ''FICA'' tax, which for 1998 amounts to 7.65% of an employee's taxable wages (a total tax of 15.3%), up to a specified amount. Self-employed persons pay the ''self-employment tax,'' which for 1998 is 15.3% of net self-employment earnings up to a specified amount. Note that self-employed workers are responsible for paying their entire social security tax liability, while employees pay only half (their employer pays the other half).

⊃ **Key point.** *Clergy always are treated as self-employed for social security purposes with respect to services performed in the exercise of their ministry,* and accordingly a minister (and his or her employing church) must not pay FICA taxes. Rather, clergy pay the self-employment tax with respect to church compensation, unless they have filed a timely application for exemption from social security taxes (and received back a copy of their exemption application from the IRS stamped ''approved''). Accordingly, clergy must be familiar with the self-employment tax rules. So must church employees who work for churches that filed an exemption from FICA coverage (Form 8274), since the effect of such an exemption is to treat all church employees as ''self-employed'' for social security purposes.

Because clergy pay a much higher social security tax than is required of employees, many churches agree to pay a portion (i.e., one-half) of a minister's self-employment tax liability. This is perfectly appropriate. However, note that any portion of a minister's self-employment tax paid by a church must be reported as additional compensation on the minister's W-2 or 1099 form, and again on the minister's Form 1040. The amount paid by the church must be reported as compensation for social security purposes as well.

⊃ **Observation.** Recent changes in the self-employment tax make it more difficult for churches wishing to pay ''half'' of a minister's self-employment tax to calculate what this amount will be. Such churches will find it much easier to simply pay a specified amount towards a minister's self-employment tax liability.

⊃ **Key point.** Housing allowances and the fair rental value of parsonages are includable in self-employment earnings for social security purposes.

**8. Insurance.** Churches often provide clergy with life, health, or disability insurance coverage and pay all of the premiums for such coverage. In some cases, churches make the same benefits available to lay staff members. The income tax regulations specify that the gross income of an *employee* does not include

contributions which his employer makes to an accident or health plan for compensation (through insurance or otherwise) to the employee for personal injuries or sickness incurred by him, his spouse, or his dependents . . . . The employer may contribute to an accident or health plan by paying the premium (or a portion of the premium) on a policy of accident or health insurance covering one or more of his employees, or by contributing to a separate trust or fund . . . .

The IRS has ruled that amounts furnished to a conference of churches by member churches to provide hospital and medical insurance coverage for clergy employees are excludable from clergy gross income under this rule.

The exclusion of employer-paid health insurance premiums from the taxable income of employees is one of the major reasons why clergy and other staff members often are better off reporting their income taxes as employees. This important benefit is not available to workers who report their income taxes as self-employed persons. A church wishing to make this benefit available to its ministers (or other employees) should adopt a plan in an appropriate board resolution. Plans that benefit only clergy are exempted from the "nondiscrimination" rules that apply to most of these kinds of plans.

> ⊃ **Observation.** The compensation survey summarized over the next several chapters reveals that many churches provide clergy with health insurance. A smaller percentage of churches provide these benefits to lay staff members. Such "discrimination" by church employers does not violate federal law.

The cost of group term life insurance bought by an employer for its employees ordinarily is not taxable to the employees so long as the amount of coverage does not exceed $50,000 per employee. Generally, life insurance can qualify as group term life insurance only if it is available to at least ten full-time employees. However, there are some exceptions to this rule. For example, the ten full-time employee rule does not apply if (1) an employer provides the insurance to all full-time employees who provide satisfactory evidence of insurability, (2) insurance coverage is based on a uniform percentage of pay, and (3) evidence of insurability is limited to a medical questionnaire completed by the employee that does not require a physical examination.

Other kinds of insurance premiums paid by the church on behalf of a minister ordinarily must be included in the minister's reportable compensation (Forms W-2, 1099, 1040). For example, the cost of premiums on a whole life or universal life insurance policy paid by a church on the life of its minister (and naming the minister's spouse and children as beneficiaries) ordinarily must be reported as income to the minister.

> ⊃ **Observation.** The compensation survey summarized over the next several chapters reveals that many churches provide clergy and lay staff members with life insurance. Note that such a benefit is taxable to the worker unless the conditions described above are satisfied. To illustrate, if a church purchases a universal life insurance policy for its minister (or any other staff member), the amount of the premiums paid by the church are taxable to the worker since this is not a group term life insurance policy of $50,000 or less.

**9. Retirement accounts.** Most clergy (and some lay staff members) participate in some form of retirement plan. Such plans often are sponsored either by the local church, or by a denomination or agency with which the church is affiliated. Church workers covered by certain kinds of plans can choose to have part of their pay set aside each year (through "salary reductions") in the retirement fund, rather than receiving it as income. Amounts set aside by the employing church under these plans may be excludable from gross income for tax purposes. These amounts are sometimes called "elective deferrals" because the employee chooses (elects) to set aside the money, and tax on the money is deferred until it is taken out of the account. This option is available to clergy or lay workers who are covered by tax-sheltered annuities ("403(b) plans"), simplified employee pensions (SEPs), and certain other plans. Payments made by an employing church toward an employee's tax-sheltered annuity, SEP, and certain other plans, and funded out of church funds rather than through a reduction in an employee's compensation, may also be excluded from the employee's gross income for tax purposes under certain circumstances. There are limits on how much an employee can elect to contribute into such plans, and on how much the employing church can contribute out of its own funds. Of course, clergy and lay workers (whether employees or self-employed for income tax purposes) can also contribute to an IRA. Self-employed workers may be eligible to establish a "Keogh account" (with higher annual contribution limits than IRAs).

➲ **Recommendation.** If a church has not established or contributed to a retirement plan for its staff members, then it should consider doing so or at least ensuring that staff members are participating in an adequate alternative (particularly in the case of clergy who have exempted themselves from social security coverage). Further, if staff members are participating in a retirement plan, then now is a good time to determine how 1997 contributions to the plan will be funded (i.e., through employee contributions, salary reductions, or church contributions), and in what amounts.

➲ **Key point.** Churches that have not adequately contributed to their minister's retirement, or that would like to make contributions in excess of applicable limits, should consider the possible advantages of a "rabbi trust." A church's contributions to such a trust will not be included in a minister's current taxable income, and income generated by the trust is tax-deferred. Further, a church ordinarily can contribute more toward a rabbi trust than to most other kinds of retirement program. This is particularly attractive for churches whose minister is approaching retirement with inadequate retirement savings. For more information see chapter 10 of Richard Hammar's *Church and Clergy Tax Guide.*

**10. Works made for hire.** Ministers and lay staff members who are authors or composers often are shocked to learn that their employing church may be the copyright owner of works that they create. Section 201 of the Copyright Act specifies that "the employer . . . is considered the author" of a "work made for hire," and "owns all of the rights comprised in the copyright" unless the employer and employee "have expressly agreed otherwise in a written instrument signed by them." The Act defines a "work made for hire" as "a work prepared by an employee within the scope of his or her employment."

To illustrate, if a minister of music composes a hymn or other musical work in his or her office in the church, during regular working hours, and using church equipment and church secretarial or clerical help, then the work almost certainly will be considered a work made for hire. The result is that the church, and not the minister, is the copyright owner. This means that the minister has no legal right in the work, and cannot enter into a contract with a publishing company for the publication and distribution of the work. The same conclusion would apply to clergy or lay workers who write articles or books.

Clergy or lay workers who produce articles, books, or musical works on church premises, using church equipment, and during regular office hours should consider entering into a written agreement with their employing church regarding copyright ownership of such works. Unless the staff member and church specifically agree otherwise in a signed writing, the copyright in such works probably will vest in the church. Of course, a staff member may be reluctant to mention this issue if the church is not aware that he or she is writing books or composing musical works during office hours. But that's the whole point. A staff member who writes articles or books or composes musical works on church equipment, using church supplies, during regular office hours, and without the church's knowledge or consent, probably should not be considered the owner of the copyright in such works. That, in any event, is the philosophy of the Copyright Act.

**11. Qualified Tuition Reductions ("QTRs").** Many churches operate elementary or secondary schools, and charge reduced tuition to certain school employees. For example, assume that First Church operates an elementary school, charges annual tuition of $1,000, but only charges tuition of $500 for the children of school employees and charges no tuition at all for the child of Rev. W (the church's senior minister and president of the school). Such "tuition reductions" are perfectly appropriate. Further, section 117(d) of the Internal Revenue Code specifies that they will not result in taxable income to the school employees. In other words, a $500 annual tuition reduction awarded to a school employee whose child attends the school need not be reported as income (on the employee's W-2 or Form 1040). This obviously can be a significant benefit to school employees. However, section 117(d) also provides that "highly compensated employees" cannot exclude qualified tuition reductions from their income unless the same benefit is available on substantially similar terms to other employees. The term "highly compensated employee" is defined to include any employee who was paid compensation for the previous year in excess of $80,000.

If in the example cited above Rev. W was paid more than $80,000 for the previous year, then the church would have to include $1,000 (the entire amount of the tuition reduction) in Rev. W's reportable income since he will be deemed a highly compensated employee, and the benefit available to him is not available on substantially similar terms to other employees. However, this will not affect other school employees who are not "highly compensated." They will be able to exclude tuition reductions from their income.

**12. Loans to clergy.** Churches often make loans to clergy to enable a minister to pay for housing or some other major purchase. Typically, the church charges no interest or a low rate far below the prevailing market rate of interest. These loans can create problems for a number of reasons. Consider the following.

    ❏ Many state nonprofit corporation laws prohibit loans to officers and directors. No church should consider making any loan (even at a reasonable rate of interest) to a minister who

17

is an officer or director of the church without first determining that such loans are permissible under state law.

☐ No-interest or low-interest loans to clergy may be viewed as "inurement" of the church's income to a minister. As noted in the preceding paragraph, this can potentially jeopardize the church's tax-exempt status.

☐ For loans of $10,000 or more (or for loans of lower amounts where an intent to avoid taxes exists), a church must value the benefit to a minister of receiving a no-interest or low-interest loan and add this amount to the minister's reportable income. This is a complex calculation that is beyond the scope of this book. The point is this—even if loans to clergy are allowed under your state's nonprofit corporation law, the church must recognize that no-interest and low-interest loans of $10,000 or more will result in income to a minister that must be valued and reported (on the minister's W-2 or 1099-MISC, and Form 1040). Failure to do so could result in prohibited "inurement" of the church's income to a private individual, and this could be disastrous for the church.

⊃ **Observation.** Sadly, some ministers and lay workers never fully repay a loan made to them by their church. The forgiveness of debt ordinarily represents taxable income to the debtor. As a result, if a church makes a loan to a minister or other staff member and the debt is later forgiven by the church, the church should report the forgiven debt as income by adding the amount to the worker's W-2 or 1099. If the worker no longer is employed by the church when the debt is forgiven, issue a corrected W-2 or 1099. A corrected W-2 is prepared on Form W-2c. Be sure to note the year of the Form W-2 that is being corrected. There is no separate form for a corrected 1099—simply fill out a new 1099 and check the box at the top of the form indicating that it is a "corrected" version.

**13. Voluntary withholding.** Compensation paid to clergy for services performed in the exercise of their ministry is not subject to either income tax or FICA withholding—and this is so whether a minister reports his or her income as an employee or as a self-employed person. Clergy are required to report and prepay their federal taxes by using the estimated tax procedure. This procedure requires clergy to estimate their income tax and self-employment tax liability for 1998 prior to April 15, 1998, and then to pay one-fourth of the total estimated tax liability on or by April 15, June 15, September 15, and the following January 15. These quarterly payments are accompanied by a "payment voucher" that is contained in IRS Form 1040-ES. Some clergy find the estimated tax procedure inconvenient and undesirable (it is often hard to budget for the quarterly payments).

Clergy who report their income taxes as employees can enter into a voluntary withholding arrangement with their employing church. Under such an arrangement, the employing church withholds income taxes as it would for any other employee, and also an additional amount for the minister's self-employment tax liability (otherwise the minister will need to use the estimated quarterly tax procedure to pay self-employment taxes). The additional amount withheld to cover self-employment taxes must be reported (on the minister's W-2 form and the church's 941 forms) as additional income tax withheld, and not as "FICA taxes." A minister need only complete and submit to his or her church an IRS Form W-4 to begin the voluntary withholding. The arrangement can be terminated by either the minister or the church at any time. Clergy who report their income taxes as self-employed could achieve the same benefit by entering into an unofficial withholding arrangement with their church under which the church withholds amounts from each paycheck to cover the minister's quarterly estimated tax payments. By each quarterly deadline, the church gives the minister the "withheld" compensation to assist him or her in making the quarterly payment. No W-4 should be prepared, since this would be evidence that the minister is in fact an employee. Churches should apprise clergy that they may enter into a voluntary withholding arrangement. For many clergy, such an arrangement will be preferable to the estimated tax procedure.

**14. Special occasion gifts.** It is common for clergy (and in some cases lay workers) to receive special occasion gifts during the course of the year. Examples include Christmas, birthday, and anniversary gifts. Churches and church staff members often do not understand how to report these payments for federal tax purposes. The general rule is this—if the "gifts" are funded through members' contributions to the church (i.e., the contributions are entered or recorded in the church's books as cash received and the members are given charitable contribution credit), then the distribution to the minister or lay worker should be reported as taxable compensation and included on his or her W-2 or 1099 and Form 1040. The same rule applies to special occasion "gifts" made to a minister or lay worker by the church out of the general fund. Members who contribute to special occasion offerings may deduct their contributions if (1) the contributions are to the church and are entered or recorded in the church's books as cash received, and (2) they are able to itemize deductions on Schedule A (Form 1040). Churches should be prepared to include such "gifts" to a minister or lay worker on his or her W-2 or 1099-MISC. Of course, members are free to make personal gifts to clergy and lay staff members, such as a card at Christmas accompanied by a check or cash. Such payments may be tax-free gifts to the recipient (though they are not deductible by the donor). These same rules apply to other kinds of special occasion gifts as well.

It is common for churches to make generous retirement gifts to retiring clergy (and in some cases lay workers). Do these gifts represent taxable income to the recipient? To the extent that the recipient is an employee (or would be classified as an employee by the IRS), there is no doubt that the "gift" would constitute taxable income. In 1986, section 102(c) was added to the Internal Revenue Code, which specifies that "any amount transferred by or for an employer to or for the benefit of an employee" shall not be excludable from gross income by the employee as a gift, other than certain employee achievement awards and insignificant holiday gifts. Those few clergy and lay workers who in fact are self-employed for income tax reporting purposes have some hope of having a retirement gift characterized as a tax-free gift rather than as taxable compensation for services rendered. Note however that such a conclusion is unlikely given the narrow definition of the term *gift*. The Supreme Court has noted that "a gift in the statutory sense . . . proceeds from a detached and disinterested generosity . . . out of affection, respect, admiration, charity, or like impulses . . . . The most critical consideration . . . is the transferor's intention." *Commissioner v. Duberstein, 363 U.S. 278, 285 (1960)*. The Court also observed that "it doubtless is the exceptional payment by an employer to an employee that amounts to a gift," and that the church's characterization of the distribution as a "gift" is "not determinative—there must be an objective inquiry as to whether what is called a gift amounts to it in reality."

⊃ *Key point. The new intermediate sanctions discussed earlier in this chapter may apply to a retirement gift that results in unreasonable compensation to the recipient. Church leaders must be sure to consider this possibility before finalizing such a gift. If a retirement gift is excessive, the board members who authorized the gift may be assessed an excise tax equal to 10 percent of the amount by which the gift exceeds reasonable compensation. This is in addition to the excise taxes that may be assessed against the recipient.*

**15. Bargain sales.** Occasionally, a church will sell property to a staff member at a price that is below market value. To illustrate, some churches "sell" a parsonage to a retiring minister at a price well below the property's fair market value. Other churches may sell a car or other church-owned vehicle to a minister at a below-market price. The important consideration with such "bargain sales" is this—the "bargain" element (i.e., the difference between the sales price charged by the church and the property's market value) must be reported as income to the minister on his or her W-2 or 1099-MISC and Form 1040. Churches should consider thoroughly the tax consequences of such sales before approving them.

**16. Director immunity.** Most states have now adopted laws that provide *uncompensated* officers and directors of most charitable organizations (including churches) with immunity from legal liability in most cases. The immunity only applies to uncompensated officers and directors. What does this have to do with compensation planning? Simply this—churches should consider adopting an appropriate resolution clarifying that a minister's annual compensation package is for ministerial duties rendered to the church, *and is not for any duties on the church board.* Like any other church officer or director, the minister serves without compensation. Such a provision, if adopted, might qualify the minister for protection under the legal immunity law. It is worth serious consideration.

**17. Discretionary funds.** It is a fairly common practice for a church to set aside a sum of money in a "discretionary fund" and give the senior minister the sole authority to distribute the money in the fund. In some cases, the minister has no instructions regarding permissible distributions. In other cases, the church establishes some guidelines, but these often are oral and ambiguous. Many churches are unaware of the tax consequences of such arrangements. To the extent the minister has the authority to use any portion of the discretionary fund for his or her own personal use, then the entire fund must be reported as taxable income to the minister in the year it is funded. This is so even if the minister in fact does not personally benefit from the fund. The mere fact that the minister *could* personally benefit from the fund is enough for the fund to constitute taxable income. The basis for this result is the "constructive receipt" rule, which is explained in the income tax regulations as follows:

> Income although not actually reduced to a taxpayer's possession is constructively received by him in the taxable year during which it is credited to his account, set apart for him, or otherwise made available so that he may draw upon it at any time, or so that he could have drawn upon it during the taxable year if notice of intention to withdraw had been given. However, income is not constructively received if the taxpayer's control of its receipt is subject to substantial limitations or restrictions.

For a discretionary fund to constitute taxable income to a minister, it is essential that the minister have the authority to "draw upon it at any time" for his or her own personal use. This means that the fund was established without any express prohibition against personal distributions. On the other hand, if a discretionary fund is set up by a board resolution that absolutely prohibits any distribution of the fund for the minister's personal use, then the constructive receipt rule is avoided. In the words of the regulation, "income is not constructively received if the taxpayer's control of its receipt is subject to substantial limitations or restrictions." Accordingly, in order to avoid the reporting of the entire discretionary fund as taxable income to the minister, it is essential that the fund be established by means of a board or congregational resolution that absolutely prohibits any use of the fund by the minister for personal purposes. Further, the resolution should specify that the fund may be distributed by the minister only for needs or projects that are consistent with the church's exempt purposes (as set forth in the church's charter). For accountability purposes, a member of the church board should review all distributions from the discretionary fund to be sure that these requirements are met.

**18. Severance pay.** Many churches have entered into severance pay arrangements with a pastor or other staff member. Such arrangements can occur when a pastor or staff member is dismissed, retires, or voluntarily resigns. Church treasurers must determine whether severance pay is taxable so that it can be properly reported (on a W-2 and the church's 941 forms). Also, taxes must be withheld from severance pay that is paid to nonminister employees (and ministers who have elected voluntary withholding). Failure to properly report severance pay can result in substantial penalties for both a church and the recipient.

In most cases severance pay represents taxable income to the recipient. There is one exception that will apply in some cases. The tax code excludes from taxable income "the amount of any damages received (whether by suit or agreement and whether as lump sums or as periodic payments) *on account of personal injuries or sickness.*" According to this provision, severance pay that is intended to settle personal injury claims may be nontaxable. The words "personal injuries" are defined broadly by the IRS and the courts, and include potential or threatened lawsuits based on discrimination and harassment.

> ⊃ **Key point.** The Tax Court has noted that "payments for terminating and canceling employment contracts are not payments for personal injuries."

Here are some factors to consider (based on actual cases) in deciding whether a severance payment made to a former worker represents taxable compensation or nontaxable damages in settlement of a personal injury claim: (1) An amount paid to a former employee "to reward her for her past services and to make her severance as amicable as possible" is taxable compensation. (2) An amount paid to a former employee under a severance agreement that contains no reference to a specific discrimination or other personal injury claim is taxable compensation. (3) If an employer pays a former employee severance pay, and reports the severance pay on a W-2 (or 1099), this is strong evidence that the amount represents taxable compensation. (4) If an employer continues one or more employee benefits (such as health insurance) as part of a severance agreement, this suggests that any amount payable under the agreement represents taxable compensation. (5) If an employer withholds taxes from amounts paid under a severance agreement, this "is a significant factor" in classifying the payments as taxable income. Of course, this factor will not be relevant in the case of ministers whose wages are not subject to withholding (unless they elect voluntary withholding). (6) Referring to a payment as "severance pay" indicates that it is taxable compensation rather than nontaxable damages in settlement of a personal injury claim. (7) Severance pay based on a former employee's salary (such as one year's salary) is more likely to be viewed as taxable compensation rather than nontaxable damages in settlement of a personal injury claim. (8) To be nontaxable, severance pay must represent "damages" received in settlement of a personal injury claim. The IRS has noted that this language requires more than a settlement agreement in which a former employee "waives" any discrimination or other personal injury claims he or she may have against an employer. If the employee "never filed a lawsuit or any other type of claim against [the employer] . . . the payment cannot be characterized as damages for personal injuries" since "there is no indication that personal injuries actually exist."

**19. Income "splitting."** Some ministers have attempted to "split" their church income with their spouse. This ordinarily is done to qualify the spouse for IRA (or pension) contributions, or to soften the impact of the social security "annual earnings test" (which reduces social security benefits to retired workers under 70 years of age who earn more than an amount prescribed by law). For income splitting arrangements to work, the courts have required proof that the spouse is in fact an employee of the church. This means that the spouse performs meaningful services on behalf of the church. The courts have pointed to a number of factors indicating that a spouse is *not* an employee: (1) The spouse did not receive a paycheck. (2) The spouse was not employed elsewhere. (3) The spouse's "compensation" was designed to provide a tax benefit (such as an IRA contribution), and lacked any economic reality. (4) Neither the church nor the minister documented any of the services the spouse performed. (5) Neither the church nor the minister could explain how the spouse's "salary" was determined. (6) There was no employment contract between the church and the minister's spouse. (7) No taxes were withheld from the spouse's "salary." (8) The spouse's income was not reported on the church's employment tax returns (Forms 941). (9) There was no evidence that wages were actually paid to the spouse, or that any employment contract existed, or that the spouse was treated as an employee.

The courts generally have been skeptical of attempts by taxpayers to shift income to a spouse. The message is clear—ministers should not attempt to obtain tax benefits by shifting income to a spouse unless there is economic reality to the arrangement.

## Compensation Checklist For 1998

| Item | Recommendations | Summary Of Action Taken |
|---|---|---|
| salary | • avoid unreasonable compensation<br>• avoid use of salary reductions that are not recognized by federal tax law | |

| | | |
|---|---|---|
| housing allowance | • for clergy who own or rent their home, designate a portion of their compensation as a housing allowance prior to December 31 for the next year<br>• for clergy who live in a church-owned parsonage, designate a portion of their compensation as a parsonage allowance (if they will incur any housing expenses) prior to December 31 for the next year | |
| equity allowance | • consider contributing to a tax-sheltered investment (such as a retirement fund) for clergy who live in church-owned parsonage, to compensate for their inability to accumulate equity in a home | |
| accountable business expense reimbursement arrangement | • adopt an accountable business expense reimbursement arrangement by reimbursing only those business expenses that are adequately substantiated, and by requiring any excess reimbursements to be returned | |
| travel expenses of a spouse | • reimburse a spouse's travel expenses incurred in accompanying a minister or lay employee on a business trip if the spouse's presence serves a legitimate business purpose and the expenses are duly substantiated (if these requirements are not met, then the church's reimbursements represent taxable income to the minister or lay employee) | |
| church-owned vehicles | • avoid allowing minister or lay employee unrestricted personal use of a church-owned car (such usage must be valued and reported as taxable income)<br>• consider adopting a policy limiting use of the car to business purposes and requiring it to be kept on church property (this avoids most recordkeeping requirements and does not result in any income to the minister)<br>• an alternative is to limit use of the car to business purposes except for commuting to and from work (if the commuting is required for security reasons); each round trip commute represents $3 of reportable income | |
| self-employment tax paid by church | • all ministers are self-employed for social security purposes with respect to their church work; this means they pay the self-employment tax rather than FICA taxes<br>• some churches pay a portion of a minister's self-employment tax (as they pay a portion of a nonminister employee's FICA taxes); such payments represent taxable income<br>• nonminister employees of churches that waived payment of FICA taxes by filing a timely Form 8274 are treated as self-employed for social security purposes—churches may want to pay a portion of the self-employment taxes owed by these workers if they do so for clergy | |
| insurance | • consider paying health insurance premiums for clergy and lay employees (a tax-free fringe benefit for employees)<br>• consider paying premiums for up to $50,000 of group term life insurance (a tax-free fringe benefit for employees) | |
| retirement accounts | • consider contributing toward a tax-sheltered retirement plan | |

| works made for hire | • consider a written action of the board acknowledging that the copyright ownership of literary or musical works created by clergy or lay employees in the course of their employment belongs to the ministers or lay employees (without such a written acknowledgment, the church owns the copyright as a "work made for hire") | |
|---|---|---|
| qualified tuition reductions | • consider tuition discounts for clergy and lay employees whose children attend church-operated schools or preschools (they may be a tax-free fringe benefit) | |
| loans to clergy | • avoid making any low or no interest loan to clergy<br>• avoid making any loan to clergy at market rates unless permitted by state nonprofit corporation law | |
| voluntary withholding | • clergy and lay workers who report their income taxes as employees should consider entering into a voluntary withholding arrangement wit the church (can avoid the quarterly estimated tax procedure); be sure to provide for the withholding of self-employment taxes too, but classify these extra withholdings as additional income taxes | |
| special occasion gifts | • special occasion gifts to clergy and lay employees that are processed through the church's books, and for which contribution credit is given to donors, are taxable income to the minister or lay employee | |
| bargain sales | • any property sold to a minister or lay employee at less than fair market value will result in taxable income (the amount by which the fair market value exceeds the sales price) | |
| director immunity | • consider adopting a board resolution certifying that all church board members, including the senior minister, serve without compensation (this may qualify the minister for the limited immunity most states provide to the uncompensated directors of nonprofit organizations) | |
| discretionary funds | • avoid them unless (1) the minister cannot use the fund for his or her own personal use, (2) the fund may be distributed only for purposes consistent with the church's exempt purposes, and (3) a board member reviews all distributions to ensure compliance with these limits | |
| severance pay | • severance pay is perfectly appropriate, but be sure that it is reported as additional taxable income unless it represents payment *on account of personal injuries or sickness* | |
| income "splitting" | • do not attempt to shift a portion of a minister's compensation to his or her spouse for tax savings purposes, unless there is "economic reality" to the arrangement (the spouse performs services that otherwise would be compensated, and receives a reasonable rate of compensation) | |

# Chapter 3

# *Using the Compensation Tables*

The following chapters present compensation patterns for nine major positions within the local church. These profiles are the statistical heart of the *Compensation Handbook*. This chapter is designed to help you interpret the tables and maximize your use of the information in this book.

Each staff position has its own chapter including both compensation tables and a discussion of the findings. The tables are for full-time staff members, except for the last table in each chapter which provides data for part-time staff members. A comparative summary of all the positions is presented in Chapter 4.

## Interpreting the Tables

Each chapter contains tables that portray compensation averages according to several key variables. The variables include the following:

- ☐ Church attendance
- ☐ Church income
- ☐ Attendance and setting[1]
- ☐ Gender
- ☐ Education
- ☐ Years employed

Each table provides several columns of averages for the following compensation items:

- ☐ Salary—annual base salary
- ☐ Annual % Increase—the percent increase of base salary for the last year.

---

1    Five settings are used: urban, suburban, medium size city, small town, rural. Each respondent was permitted to use his or her own judgment in defining their setting. The same approach is followed in using the tables. Each user must determine his or her own setting.

- ☐ Parsonage—rental value of parsonage plus other housing expenses.

- ☐ Housing—amount of housing allowance provided for the purchase or rent of a home and its up-keep and furnishings.

- ☐ Retirement—money church provides for retirement, not including social security payments.

- ☐ Life Insurance—cost of life insurance provided for staff member as a benefit.

- ☐ Health Insurance—cost of health insurance provided for staff member as a benefit.

- ☐ Vacation/weeks—number of weeks of paid vacation.

- ☐ Auto Allowance—auto allowance is included as part of the base salary. Each table, however, lists the percentage of staff members receiving an auto allowance.

- ☐ Education Funds—amount provided for continuing education.

Immediately following the listing for the compensation item is a percentage. That percentage indicates the proportion of staff members who receive that benefit. For example, consider the following example taken from Chapter 5:

---

### Table 5-3: Annual Compensation Of Senior Pastors By Church Setting And Size

| Attendance 0-250 | Urban | Suburban | Medium City | Small Town | Rural |
|---|---|---|---|---|---|
| Number of Respondents | 87 | 205 | 140 | 248 | 89 |
| Salary (99%) | 28,002 | 28,487 | 27,032 | 25,741 | 21,907 |
| Annual % Increase (65%) | 6% | 6% | 6% | 5% | 5% |
| Parsonage (20%) | 11,817 | 14,384 | 8,258 | 6,429 | 6,881 |

---

Notice that (99%) follows *Salary*. This indicates that 99% of the respondents received a salary. The other 1% received their compensation in other ways, For example, a pastor of a small church may receive his or her total compensation as a housing allowance and fringe benefits. Following *Parsonage* is (20%). This means that 20% of all senior pastors lived in a church provided parsonage. In the first column on the *Parsonage* line is the figure 11,817. This means that of the 20% of all senior pastors who received a parsonage allowance, those that serve urban churches with an attendance between 0-250 received on average an allowance of $11,817.

## Total Compensation Comparisons

Below each table is a smaller box that lists the *average compensation* for each category. The *average compensation* includes the sum of the base salary, the housing or parsonage allowance, retirement contributions, life and health insurance payments, and educational funds. *This is the key figure for compensation analysis.* The following information is also found in the *Total Compensation Comparisons* box.

## Standard Deviation

Following the average compensation is the standard deviation. The standard deviation is the most important and widely used measure of dispersion. In a normal distribution, one standard deviation away from the average represents 68.27% of all responses. For example, in this study the average compensation for pastors was $56,172. The standard deviation was $23,705. Thus, approximately 68% of all pastors receive a compensation falling between $32,467 (56,172 - 23,705) and $79,877 (56,172 + 23,705). A range of two standard deviations on either side of the average encompasses 95% of responses.

## National Average

Included in the *Total Compensation Comparisons* box is the national average. This figure represents the average compensation nationwide for that position.

## Rounding Errors

Rounding errors may exist in some of the data in this study. They do not, however, impact the final results in any significant way. Some of the hourly wages for part-time workers may deviate a few cents due to rounding errors.

# Using the Tables To Plan Compensation

The most important use of this handbook is for compensation planning. The following example illustrates one approach of how this book can be used.

## Example: Planning the Compensation of a Senior Pastor

> *Reverend West has served as senior pastor of Maywood Church for the past sixteen years. Maywood Church is a suburban congregation with an average Sunday worship attendance of 650, and an annual budget of $742,000. Reverend West has a Master of Divinity degree.*

*Step 1.* The first step is to use the Tables in Chapter 5 to identify the average compensation for senior pastors according to church (1) attendance, (2) budget, and (3) size and setting (urban, suburban, medium size city, small town, rural). To collect this information we examine the data in Table 5-1, Table 5-2, and Table 5-5. The figures below are taken from those Tables.

| | | | | |
|---|---|---|---|---|
| **attendance (Table 5-1):** | *650* | **average compensation:** | *$67,131* | *(for an average attendance of 589)* |
| **budget (Table 5-2):** | *$742,000* | **average compensation:** | *$65,066* | *(for an average budget of $600,471)* |
| **setting (Table 5-5):** | *suburban* | **average compensation:** | *$68,210* | *(for an average attendance of 628)* |

The data from these three tables provide us with a range of average compensation between $65,066 to $68,210. These figures serve as an average base compensation range. **Note:** *these figures do not take into account differences in the cost of living from one part of the country to another.*

*Step 2.* The second step is to examine additional factors that might impact compensation such as *education* and *years of service*. This requires an examination of Table 5-9 (*Annual Compensation Of Senior Pastors By Education*) and Table 5-10 (*Annual Compensation Of Senior Pastors By Years Employed*). In Table 5-9 we note in the *Total Compensation Comparisons* box that a master's degree is about the same as the national average ($56,798 compared to $56,172). If our senior pastor had a doctorate degree, for example, a differential would exist.

For our example, the senior pastor has served in the church for 16 years. Table 5-10 indicates that the average compensation for pastors serving over 15 years is $66,023 which is about 17% above the national average. However, the average number of years employed for this figure is 22 years, well over the 16 years of our pastor. This, however, is not too significant because those with 13 years average service earn $57,486, or only about 2% above the national average. Thus we might expect our pastor to earn slightly above the national average based upon his years of service. The question is whether the increase is due to years of service or other factors as noted in step 3. (We might also do the same process with the denominational data found in Chapter 4).

*Step 3.* In this step we make adjustments, if needed, based on the analysis from step 2. In examining the years of service found in Table 5-10 we note that the average church size for the group was 614 and average budget was $882,236. These figures are similar to those in our example. Thus we may conclude that no adjustment is needed based on years of service. The figure of $66,023 in Table 5-10 falls within our already established range.

*Step 4.* The fourth step is to take into account the unique circumstances that define your situation. One factor is the cost of living for your area. Is it higher or lower than the national average?. Your local Chamber of Commerce can help you obtain that information. Other factors such as theological beliefs, pastoral performance, financial needs, goodwill, the local economy, personal motivation, congregational goals, internal church politics, and many other considerations will also contribute to the final decision. For some churches that may mean a final compensation package much lower or much higher than our projected range listed in Step 3. The average church, however, will be fairly close to that range. How that compensation will be divided up will vary greatly from one church to another, and even from one individual staff member to another. Care should be given, however, to avoid gender discrimination. This is a widespread problem involving many churches.

*Step 5.* The final step is to examine the *standard deviation* range for senior pastors. Use Table 4-3 found in Chapter 4. That table indicates that the compensation of 95% of all pastors is less than $103,582 and that 68% of pastors earn less than $79,877. Thus the projected compensation for our pastor, considering personal background and the profile of the church, is well within the typical range. The primary concern is to make certain that the final compensation total does not fall so far outside of the normal distribution of clergy compensation that the church could possibly lose its tax exempt status due to payments that the tax court might consider "unreasonable" (see the discussion on *Salary* in Chapter 2).

This same process can be used for each of the nine staff positions found in this handbook.

# Chapter 4

# *Compensation Profiles: General Comparisons*

This chapter provides comparisons of the average compensations for the nine staff positions included in this study. A summary table exists for each of the variables examined. More detailed analysis can be found in the individual chapter for each staff position.

As expected, pastors consistently rank first in total compensation for church staff members. Associate pastors received the second highest compensation amount followed generally by music and choir directors. The tables presented later in this chapter provide compensation rankings and comparisons according to the national averages for each position.

## What factors determine compensation?

Size, setting, budget, and gender were the four most important factors affecting total compensation. While no single factor played the decisive role, female staff members consistently received lower compensation than did their male counterparts.

Church income and attendance proved to be the most important variables affecting compensation for each of the nine positions examined in this study. Yet, the correlation between these variables and employee compensation accounts for only a small percentage of the variation in compensation amounts for these positions. To say that the size of the church's budget or attendance determines compensation is both wrong and misleading. These factors, while important, must be viewed in the context of other factors, the combination of which ultimately determine compensation. For example, theology may play a significant role in some churches in the determination of compensation. The compensation of a Catholic priest who has taken a vow of poverty will be low regardless of church size or income. In churches that promote financial prosperity as a sign of God's blessing, the pastor may receive a disproportionate amount of the church's total income. Politics and power may prove the decisive factors in determining compensation in a church embroiled in conflict. A building program may be the controlling factor somewhere else. In general, education, geographical setting, and years of service play some role in almost every church. Unfortunately, significant gender gaps existed for every position except church secretary where 99% of the employees were female. While some of these gaps can be explained on the basis of demographic factors such as church setting or personal education, the conclusion cannot be escaped that gender discrimination is widespread within the church concerning compensation and the access to higher paying positions. The largest compensation gap between men and women was for church administrators—on average, for this position, men earned 39% more than women. The earning gap also was 30% or higher for CE directors and music/choir directors.

# General Trends

This study examined the "rate of increase" with respect to compensation and church attendance, and compensation and church budget. In this context, "rate of increase" refers to how fast compensation rose with respect to church attendance or size of church budget. For most staff positions, the rate of increase for total compensation was the highest for churches with an attendance over 200. This was especially true for pastors, associate pastors, music and choir directors, and CE directors. Compensation for these positions tended to level off or slow down once the church reached an attendance of 500. It picked up once again once attendance passed the 750 mark with pastors and church administrators experiencing the largest gains.

Church bookkeepers, secretaries, and custodians experienced only modest compensation growth increase as the church size increased. Like the other positions, compensation tended to flatten out for churches with an attendance between 200 to 750. Some compensation growth appeared for larger churches, but even then, their total compensation was considerably less than the other church staff positions.

Similar trends could be seen based upon church budgets. Pastoral compensation increased at every budget level, but the rate of growth was the slowest for congregations with budgets between $300,000 and $600,000. The same was true for associate pastors, music/choir directors, and CE directors. Youth ministers experience only modest increases in compensation once the church budget hits $750,000. Bookkeepers, secretaries, and custodians did not fare as well. Bookkeepers and secretaries experienced little growth until the budget exceeded $800,000. Custodians began to receive more compensation more quickly as church budgets approached $400,000. Their income actually declined slightly once the budget exceeded $500,000 and then increased again once the budget exceeded $750,000.

# Benefit Comparison

Benefits vary significantly from one position to the next. This was especially true for the more important benefits of health insurance and retirement programs. Only 43-79 percent of church staff have health insurance and fewer have retirement benefits. Bookkeepers, custodians, and secretaries are less likely to receive benefits than are the other professional staff members. Part-time staff members receive few fringe benefits. The tables below provide benefit comparisons (please note that some position titles and benefit listings have been abbreviated).

## Table 4-1: Percentage of Full-time Staff Receiving Benefits

|  | Pastor | Associate | CE Dir. | Youth | Music | Admin. | Book. | Secretary | Custodian |
|---|---|---|---|---|---|---|---|---|---|
| raise | 65% | 68% | 68% | 66% | 69% | 67% | 69% | 67% | 63% |
| parsonage | 20% | 9% | 2% | 6% | 1% | 1% | 0% | 0% | 1% |
| housing | 81% | 86% | 58% | 68% | 57% | 23% | 2% | 0% | 1% |
| retirement | 70% | 63% | 57% | 52% | 54% | 44% | 32% | 26% | 27% |
| life ins. | 31% | 30% | 29% | 28% | 32% | 28% | 29% | 18% | 22% |
| health ins. | 77% | 79% | 72% | 76% | 72% | 60% | 50% | 43% | 52% |
| vacation | 95% | 94% | 93% | 94% | 94% | 94% | 92% | 89% | 88% |
| auto allow. | 68% | 74% | 75% | 76% | 74% | 73% | 66% | 14% | 60% |
| education | 44% | 45% | 46% | 36% | 38% | 32% | 14% | 14% | 4% |

## Table 4-2: Percentage of Part-time Staff Receiving Benefits

|  | Pastor | Associate | CE Dir. | Youth | Music | Admin. | Book. | Secretary | Custodian |
|---|---|---|---|---|---|---|---|---|---|
| raise | 36% | 35% | 57% | 36% | 50% | 59% | 52% | 53% | 45% |
| parsonage | 23% | 4% | 1% | 2% | 0% | 0% | 0% | 0% | 0% |
| housing | 52% | 40% | 8% | 10% | 3% | 8% | 1% | 0% | 0% |
| retirement | 32% | 19% | 5% | 7% | 4% | 13% | 6% | 5% | 2% |
| life ins. | 11% | 9% | 4% | 5% | 2% | 3% | 3% | 2% | 1% |
| health ins. | 23% | 20% | 13% | 13% | 4% | 12% | 6% | 6% | 4% |
| vacation | 70% | 49% | 52% | 38% | 42% | 53% | 37% | 49% | 30% |
| auto allow. | 61% | 61% | 53% | 51% | 41% | 52% | 45% | 41% | 35% |
| education | 27% | 24% | 23% | 18% | 15% | 12% | 7% | 8% | 1% |

## Note: the following tables are for comparative purposes only. For a full analysis of each staff position, consult chapters 5-13.

### Table 4-3: National Church Staff Compensation Averages

| Position | Average Compensation* | Standard Deviation | $\overline{X} \pm 1$ (68%) | $\overline{X} \pm 2$ (95%) |
|---|---|---|---|---|
| Pastor | 56,172 | 23,705 | 32,467 - 79,877 | 8,762 -103,582 |
| Associate Pastor | 45,052 | 16,134 | 28918 - 61,186 | 12,784 - 77,320 |
| Music Choir Dir. | 43,598 | 15,653 | 27,945 - 59,251 | 12,292 - 74,904 |
| Administrator | 37,413 | 16,373 | 21,040 - 53,786 | 4,667 - 70,159 |
| CE Director | 40,863 | 15,408 | 25,455 - 56,271 | 10,047 - 71,679 |
| Youth Minister | 36,968 | 12,494 | 24,474 - 49,462 | 11,980 - 61,956 |
| Bookkeeper | 23,839 | 7,890 | 15,949 - 31,729 | 8,059 - 39,619 |
| Custodian | 22,493 | 8,983 | 13,510 - 31,476 | 4,527 - 40,459 |
| Secretary | 20,232 | 6,467 | 13,765 - 26,699 | 7,298 - 33,166 |

* The average compensation includes base salary (including auto allowance), housing or parsonage allowance, retirement contribution, life and health insurance payments, and educational funds.

## Using the Standard Deviation

In a normal distribution, one standard deviation away from the average represents 68.27% of all responses. For example, in this study the average compensation for pastors was $56,172. The standard deviation was $23,705. Thus, approximately 68% of all pastors receive a compensation falling between $32,467 (56,172 minus 23,705) and $79,877 (56,172 plus 23,705)). A range of two standard deviations on either side of the average encompasses 95% of responses. The standard deviations listed in the table above apply only to national averages for each position and not to the other tables in this chapter.

### Table 4-4: Annual Church Staff Compensation Averages By Church Attendance*

| Attendance | 0-99 | 100-299 | 300-499 | 500-749 | 750-999 | over 1,000 |
|---|---|---|---|---|---|---|
| Pastor | 36,699 | 48,358 | 58,960 | 67,131 | 74,975 | 86,310 |
| Associate Pastor | 20,579 | 33,578 | 42,997 | 49,147 | 49,682 | 54,353 |
| CE Director | 0 | 30,928 | 35,890 | 40,613 | 42,451 | 50,178 |
| Youth Minister | 0 | 29,205 | 35,021 | 38,049 | 39,433 | 44,624 |
| Music/Choir Dir. | 0 | 28,731 | 38,542 | 43,008 | 47.472 | 52,141 |
| Administrator | 22,282 | 23,829 | 29,720 | 35,290 | 41,237 | 51,487 |
| Bookkeeper | 0 | 20,002 | 20,494 | 23,119 | 22,857 | 27,531 |
| Secretary | 18,594 | 18,308 | 19,565 | 20,778 | 22,192 | 23,712 |
| Custodian | 0 | 17,114 | 21,049 | 22,809 | 23,525 | 26,251 |

* The average compensation includes base salary (including auto allowance), housing or parsonage allowance, retirement contribution, life and health insurance payments, and educational funds.

### Table 4-5: Annual Church Staff Compensation Averages By Church Income*

| Church Budget in $ | 0-249,999 | 250,000-499,999 | 500,000-749,000 | 750,000-999,999 | 1,000,000 + |
|---|---|---|---|---|---|
| Pastor | 43,457 | 54,482 | 65,066 | 68,584 | 85,531 |
| Associate Pastor | 27,864 | 39,686 | 45,460 | 50,734 | 54,944 |
| CE Director | 29,491 | 31,162 | 34,806 | 40,348 | 47,973 |
| Youth Minister | 26,943 | 32,408 | 35,135 | 41,359 | 42,855 |
| Music/Choir Dir. | 22,993 | 31,346 | 38,572 | 39,952 | 51,805 |
| Administrator | 22,031 | 26,493 | 31,822 | 36,491 | 48,982 |
| Bookkeeper | 18,041 | 20,479 | 19,913 | 23,665 | 26,648 |
| Secretary | 17,019 | 19,559 | 21,356 | 20,395 | 23,626 |
| Custodian | 15,170 | 17,549 | 21,862 | 22,160 | 26,094 |

* The average compensation includes base salary (including auto allowance), housing or parsonage allowance, retirement contribution, life and health insurance payments, and educational funds.

## Table 4-6: Annual Church Staff Compensation Averages By Church Setting And Size*

| Attendance Under 500 | Urban | Suburban | Medium City | Small Town | Rural |
|---|---|---|---|---|---|
| Pastor | 50,996 | 55,419 | 50,126. | 44,116 | 37,982 |
| Associate Pastor | 40,671 | 43,205 | 36,896 | 32,228 | 28,418 |
| CE Director | 33,719 | 37,212 | 33,566 | 31,556 | 25,236 |
| Youth Minister | 29,956 | 36,537 | 32,732 | 27,263 | 29,953 |
| Music/Choir Dir. | 35,020 | 35,185 | 40,522 | 30,899 | 24,298 |
| Administrator | 27,201 | 30,046 | 27,116 | 24,159 | 18,823 |
| Bookkeeper | 19,414 | 21,946 | 21,933 | 18,556 | 15,600 |
| Secretary | 20,910 | 20,428 | 18,545 | 17,068 | 16,044 |
| Custodian | 21,770 | 22,003 | 18,855 | 16,077 | 10,900 |

* The average compensation includes base salary (including auto allowance), housing or parsonage allowance, retirement contribution, life and health insurance payments, and educational funds.

## Table 4-7: Annual Church Staff Compensation Averages By Church Setting And Size*

| Attendance over 499 | Urban | Suburban | Medium City | Small Town | Rural |
|---|---|---|---|---|---|
| Pastor | 81,389 | 78,727 | 68,856 | 64,861 | 65,568 |
| Associate Pastor | 54,299 | 53,782 | 48,814 | 43,883 | 53,494 |
| CE Director | 44,872 | 47,087 | 43,280 | 39,143 | 0 |
| Youth Minister | 37,849 | 43,505 | 38,878 | 38,140 | 41,488 |
| Music/Choir Dir. | 49,945 | 48,836 | 47,617 | 42,357 | 44,516 |
| Administrator | 46,804 | 49,173 | 36,458 | 41,808 | 39,266 |
| Bookkeeper | 27,236 | 26,770 | 23,022 | 21,073 | 23,747 |
| Secretary | 23,605 | 23,147 | 20,915 | 20,112 | 19,686 |
| Custodian | 25,516 | 25,145 | 23,041 | 23,143 | 21,514 |

* The average compensation includes base salary (including auto allowance), housing or parsonage allowance, retirement contribution, life and health insurance payments, and educational funds.

## Table 4-8: Annual Church Staff Compensation Averages By Gender *

| Gender | Male | Female | Earning Gap |
|---|---|---|---|
| Pastor | 56,431 | 46,269 | 18% |
| Associate Pastor | 45,777 | 38,242 | 16% |
| CE Director | 47,047 | 32,537 | 31% |
| Youth Minister | 37,592 | 29,085 | 23% |
| Music/Choir Dir. | 46,020 | 30,646 | 33% |
| Administrator | 45,394 | 27,845 | 39% |
| Bookkeeper | 27,176 | 23,517 | 13% |
| Secretary | 19,170 | 20,282 | 5% |
| Custodian | 23,433 | 16,815 | 28% |

* The average compensation includes base salary (including auto allowance), housing or parsonage allowance, retirement contribution, life and health insurance payments, and educational funds.

## Table 4-9: Annual Church Staff Compensation Averages By Education*

| Highest Degree | High School | Associate | Bachelor | Master | Doctorate |
|---|---|---|---|---|---|
| Pastor | 43,561 | 45,417 | 50,076 | 56,798 | 68,552 |
| Associate Pastor | 34,285 | 36,809 | 41,795 | 48,073 | 58,954 |
| CE Director | 25,584 | 35,065 | 36,820 | 46,770 | 59,954 |
| Youth Minister | 29,444 | 34,913 | 35,618 | 42,169 | 49,597 |
| Music/Choir Dir. | 37,716 | 34,721 | 42,832 | 49,481 | 51,857 |
| Administrator | 27,301 | 30,668 | 38,825 | 47,487 | 42,864 |
| Bookkeeper | 24,453 | 21,723 | 25,608 | 21,760 | 0 |
| Secretary | 19,864 | 19,771 | 21,395 | 20,598 | 0 |
| Custodian | 22,535 | 22,307 | 26,339 | 22,554 | 0 |

* The average compensation includes base salary (including auto allowance), housing or parsonage allowance, retirement contribution, life and health insurance payments, and educational funds.

## Table 4-10: Annual Church Staff Compensation Averages By Years Employed*

| Years Employed | 0-5 | 6-10 | 11-15 | over 15 |
|---|---|---|---|---|
| Pastor | 51,387 | 57,910 | 57,486 | 66,023 |
| Associate Pastor | 41,255 | 49,536 | 51,580 | 56,156 |
| CE Director | 40,040 | 42,286 | 39,772 | 49,383 |
| Youth Minister | 35,522 | 42,214 | 46,275 | 50,238 |
| Music/Choir Dir. | 42,191 | 45,045 | 45,500 | 50,860 |
| Administrator | 35,841 | 37,181 | 40,024 | 45,612 |
| Bookkeeper | 23,475 | 23,513 | 24,630 | 25,782 |
| Secretary | 19,296 | 20,708 | 21,725 | 21,989 |
| Custodian | 21,879 | 22,495 | 24,017 | 28,308 |

* The average compensation includes base salary (including auto allowance), housing or parsonage allowance, retirement contribution, life and health insurance payments, and educational funds.

## Table 4-11: Annual Hourly Compensation Averages For Part-Time Church Staff*

| Hours per week | 1-14 | 15-29 | 30-39 | All Part-time |
|---|---|---|---|---|
| Pastor | 0 | 8.28 | 12.41 | 12.03 |
| Associate Pastor | 20.91 | 13.50 | 17.86 | 15.42 |
| CE Director | 17.11 | 11.47 | 14.53 | 12.81 |
| Youth Minister | 12.50 | 9.86 | 10.41 | 10.39 |
| Music/Choir Dir. | 17.13 | 16.83 | 15.06 | 14.23 |
| Administrator | 8.85 | 12.06 | 12.74 | 11.24 |
| Bookkeeper | 12.09 | 9.27 | 10.46 | 8.92 |
| Secretary | 12.22 | 8.15 | 9.45 | 9.12 |
| Custodian | 10.79 | 8.39 | 8.50 | 8.67 |

* The average compensation includes base salary (including auto allowance), housing or parsonage allowance, retirement contribution, life and health insurance payments, and educational funds. Not all part-time staff persons indicated the number of hours worked.

# Table 4-12: Denominational Compensation Comparisons*

| | Pastor | As. Pastor | CE Dir. | Youth | Choir | Admin. | Book. | Sec. | Custodian |
|---|---|---|---|---|---|---|---|---|---|
| A/G (134) ** | 52,597 | 34,322 | 37,592 | 30,463 | 39,658 | 32,298 | 22,481 | 17,724 | 24,445 |
| Baptist (367) | 55,961 | 46,215 | 47,499 | 39,950 | 46,554 | 45,920 | 21,904 | 19,505 | 21,502 |
| Brethren (13) | 51,275 | | | | | | | | |
| Catholic (13) | 29,698 | | | | 33,035 | 33,906 | | 22,807 | 23,312 |
| Christian (28) | 41,872 | 39,152 | | 36,061 | | | | | |
| CMA (25) | 49,292 | 39,962 | | 37,639 | | | | 20,677 | |
| Ch of Christ (22) | 47,772 | 42,284 | | 33,488 | | | | 16,706 | |
| Ch of God (23) | 54,911 | | | 36,945 | 47,555 | | | 20,362 | 22,667 |
| Covenant (11) | 60,157 | | | 39,944 | | | | | |
| Episcopal (38) | 66,394 | 57,218 | | 35,587 | | 33,707 | | 21,188 | 25,580 |
| Evang. Free (37) | 57,530 | 48,001 | | 46,249 | 46,835 | 46,090 | | 22,308 | 27,562 |
| Independent (75) | 55,059 | 46,457 | 40,314 | 42,481 | 46,391 | 40,192 | 25,748 | 21,280 | 27,092 |
| Lutheran (119) | 58,464 | 49,277 | 51,406 | 38,436 | 40,045 | | 23,324 | 20,794 | 22,406 |
| Nazarene (18) | 49,030 | 43,120 | | 32,401 | | | | 20,706 | |
| Nondenom. (183) | 54,577 | 44,597 | 42,574 | 35,741 | 42,567 | 39,752 | 25,974 | 20,090 | 21,726 |
| Presbyterian (100) | 65,090 | 54,305 | 37,405 | 36,000 | 48,367 | 39,477 | 25,676 | 23,757 | 22,749 |
| Reformed (10) | 67,445 | | | 41,550 | | | | | |
| UCC (58) | 56,038 | 38,546 | 34,116 | 43,593 | | 23,415 | | 21,536 | 21,482 |
| United Meth. (97) | 65,567 | 44,020 | 32,532 | 29,047 | 37,762 | 32,717 | 26,302 | 19,052 | 19,133 |
| Other*** (239) | 51,536 | 44,836 | 37,684 | 38,607 | 32,952 | 31,649 | 20,850 | 19,556 | 27,419 |
| | | | | | | | | | |
| National Average | 56,172 | 45,052 | 40,863 | 36,968 | 43,598 | 37,413 | 23,839 | 20,232 | 22,493 |

* The average compensation includes base salary (including auto allowance), housing or parsonage allowance, retirement contribution, life and health insurance payments, and educational funds.

** The number in parentheses following the denominational listing indicates the number of senior pastors reporting from that denomination. Blank spaces in the columns for other staff members indicates less than 10 respondents. Refer to "Other" at the bottom of the table.

*** Includes all other denominations with less than 10 respondents..

# Chapter 5

# *Senior Pastors*

## Employment Profile

Senior pastors provided a significant number of responses to this survey with 1,547 participants. This group was composed of both pastors who oversee a multiple staff including other clergy and individual pastors who are the only ordained employee of their church. As can be expected, this group is quite diverse. Significant differences exist in training, church size, church income, and years served. Over 97% of the pastors surveyed serve full-time. The following statistical features profile this sample:

|  | Full-time | Part-time |
|---|---|---|
| ☐ Number of Respondents | 1,503 | 44 |
| ☐ Ordained | 99% | 93% |
| ☐ Average years employed | 9 | 6 |
| ☐ Male | 98% | 93% |
| ☐ Female | 2% | 7% |
| ☐ Self-employed | 10% | 39% |
| ☐ Church Employee | 90% | 61% |
| ☐ Senior pastor of multiple staff | 69% | 66% |
| ☐ Solo pastor | 31% | 34% |
| ☐ High School Diploma | 4% | 15% |
| ☐ Associate Degree | 4% | 3% |
| ☐ Bachelor Degree | 27% | 24% |
| ☐ Master Degree | 42% | 45% |
| ☐ Doctorate | 23% | 13% |

## Compensation Analysis

The analysis below is based upon the tables found later in this chapter. The tables present compensation data for pastors who serve full-time according to church attendance, church income, combinations of size and setting, gender, education, and years employed. The final table provides data for part-time pastors based upon the number of hours worked. In this way, the pastor's compensation can be analyzed and compared from a variety of useful perspectives. The total compensation amount was calculated by adding the base salary (including auto allowance), housing or parsonage amount, retirement contribution, life and health insurance payments, and educational funds.

## Key Points

✎ *Church income had the strongest correlation with compensation.* Yet, the correlation is not a strong one and must be considered as only one of many factors that determined compensation. As the church's income increased, compensation went up. Pastors in churches with budgets over $300,000 tended to be equal to or above the national average compensation. Pastors serving churches with incomes over $1,000,000 received on average almost twice the compensation of a pastor in a church with a budget under $250,000. *See Table 5-2.*

✎ *Church attendance affected pastoral compensation.* Of the pastors surveyed, 55% worked in churches with an average attendance under 300 people. The compensation of these pastors was below the national average. Compensation increases significantly as attendance moves between 200 to 300. The average number of years served tends to increase slightly as attendance increases. *See Table 5-1.*

✎ *A church's geographical setting affected pastoral compensation.* Pastors of suburban churches continue to have the highest compensation for churches under 250 in attendance. Historically, urban pastors have the highest for churches over 250 in attendance, and with an exception for Table 5-6, that trend continued in 1997. Generally, speaking, churches located in urban, suburban and medium size cities provided higher housing allowances, retirement contributions, and insurance payments, although health insurance payments were often comparable. *See Tables 5-3, 5-4, 5-5, 5-6 and 5-7.*

✎ *Significant gender disparities exist concerning pastoral compensation.* On average, female pastors earned 82% of their male counterparts, the same as last year. At this time, women do not have access to larger churches. The average congregational size that men serve is 427 people, while for women it is 193. These differences in congregational size represent a corresponding difference in church income of over $200,000. *See Table 5-8.*

✎ *A relationship existed between educational achievement and income for pastors.* Pastors with only a high school diploma earned over $6,000 less than pastors with a bachelor's degree. In general, only those with a graduate degree reached the national average. The biggest increase in compensation occurred when a pastor obtained a doctoral degree. These individuals were more likely to serve larger urban or suburban churches which provided the highest levels of compensation. Average years employed was almost identical regardless of educational background. Over 90% of the respondents were college graduates and 65% had graduate degrees. The most common was a master's degree held by 42% of those responding to this survey. Over 20% held doctoral degrees. *See Table 5-9.*

✎ *Years of service has some impact on compensation.* Those serving for less than five years in their current position (45% of the respondents) received over $14,000 a year less in total compensation than those who had served over 15 years. The difference, however, appears to be more dependent on church income than on years served. Those serving the longest tended to be in bigger churches with significantly higher incomes. *See Table 5-10.*

✎ **On average, part-time pastors worked 25 hours per week for their church.** Nearly all part-time pastors served churches with an average attendance under 200 people. Their tenure was about three years less than that of full-time pastors. Comparatively, compensation was significantly less for part-time pastors than those serving full-time. *See Table 5-11.*

# Benefit Analysis

**Full-time staff members.** The pastor was the most highly paid position in the local church and received the best benefits. Most pastors own or rent a home. Slightly over three-fourths of pastors received health insurance and 70% had retirement benefits.

**Part-time staff members.** Less than 3% of the pastors in this survey served their church on a part-time basis. Part-time pastors received fewer benefits than full-time pastors in every compensation category.

| Benefits | Full-time | Part-time |
|---|---|---|
| ❏ Housing allowance | 81% | 52% |
| ❏ Parsonage provided | 20% | 23% |
| ❏ Retirement | 70% | 32% |
| ❏ Health insurance | 77% | 23% |
| ❏ Life insurance | 31% | 11% |
| ❏ Paid vacation | 95% | 70% |
| ❏ Auto allowance | 68% | 61% |
| ❏ Continuing education expenses | 44% | 27% |

# Five Year Compensation Trend: National Averages for Pastors

| | |
|---|---|
| ❏ 1993 | $49,536 |
| ❏ 1994 | $50,400 |
| ❏ 1995 | $51,592 |
| ❏ 1996 | $55,027 |
| ❏ 1997 | $56,172 |

## Table 5-1: Annual Compensation Of Senior Pastor By Worship Attendance

| Church Attendance | 0-99 | 100-299 | 300-499 | 500-749 | 750-999 | 1,000+ |
|---|---|---|---|---|---|---|
| Number Of Respondents | 179 | 622 | 274 | 166 | 86 | 130 |
| Salary (99%*) | 21,854 | 27,614 | 34,292 | 38,124 | 45,372 | 51,065 |
| Annual % Increase (65%) | 7% | 5% | 5% | 5% | 5% | 5% |
| Parsonage (20%) | 6,612 | 9,801 | 17,556 | 20,383 | 13,819 | 19,122 |
| Housing (81%) | 11,045 | 14,328 | 17,543 | 20,652 | 21,316 | 26,489 |
| Retirement (70%) | 2,920 | 3,983 | 4,431 | 4,811 | 5,151 | 6,474 |
| Life Insurance (31%) | 1,456 | 1,256 | 930 | 1,012 | 948 | 1,199 |
| Health Insurance (77%) | 4,025 | 4,752 | 5,334 | 5,121 | 5,275 | 5,543 |
| Vacation/weeks (95%) | 3 | 3 | 4 | 4 | 4 | 4 |
| Education Funds (44%) | 1,014 | 1,009 | 1,258 | 1,365 | 1,325 | 2,295 |
| Receive Auto Allow.(68%) | 50% | 61% | 73% | 79% | 86% | 82% |

* The percentage following each compensation item indicates the portion of all senior pastors who received that form of compensation. The averages in each column are for those individuals who actually received that compensation item. Auto allowance is included as part of base salary. See Chapter  for a full explanation of how to read this table.

## Total Compensation Comparisons

| Church Attendance | 0-99 | 100-299 | 300-499 | 500-749 | 750-999 | 1,000+ |
|---|---|---|---|---|---|---|
| Average attendance | 68 | 182 | 372 | 589 | 842 | 1,666 |
| Average church income | 90,135 | 221,103 | 488,266 | 816,287 | 1,160,128 | 2,148,154 |
| Average years employed | 6 | 8 | 8 | 9 | 11 | 13 |
| Average compensation* | 36,699 | 48,358 | 58,960 | 67,131 | 74,975 | 86,310 |
| Standard deviation | 19,327 | 17,656 | 21,035 | 22,894 | 17,497 | 45,791 |

National average for all senior pastors: $56,172 with a standard deviation of $23,705 (see Chapter 4, Table 4-3).

Total respondents: 1,457

* includes base salary, housing or parsonage allowance, retirement contribution, life and health insurance payments, and educational funds (note: auto allowance is included in base salary).

## Table 5-2: Annual Compensation Of Senior Pastor By Church Income

| Church Income in $ | 0-249,999 | 250,000-499,999 | 500,000-749,000 | 750,000-999,999 | 1,000,000 + |
|---|---|---|---|---|---|
| Number Of Respondents | 575 | 332 | 154 | 78 | 212 |
| Salary (99%*) | 25,453 | 31,036 | 38,397 | 37,713 | 50,003 |
| Annual % Increase (65%) | 6% | 6% | 5% | 5% | 5% |
| Parsonage (20%) | 8,352 | 12,138 | 24,498 | 16,150 | 20,278 |
| Housing (81%) | 12,566 | 16,584 | 17,525 | 22,559 | 25,768 |
| Retirement (70%) | 3,569 | 4,264 | 4,804 | 5,423 | 6,193 |
| Life Insurance (31%) | 1,396 | 847 | 971 | 1,034 | 1,105 |
| Health Insurance (77%) | 4,415 | 5,148 | 5,308 | 5,327 | 5,540 |
| Vacation/weeks (95%) | 3 | 4 | 4 | 4 | 4 |
| Education Funds (44%) | 948 | 1,201 | 1,344 | 1,356 | 1,916 |
| Receive Auto Allow.(68%) | 56% | 67% | 74% | 81% | 86% |

* The percentage following each compensation item indicates the portion of all senior pastors who received that form of compensation. The averages in each column are for those individuals who actually received that compensation item. Auto allowance is included as part of base salary. See Chapter for a full explanation of how to read this table.

## Total Compensation Comparisons

| Church Income | 0-249,999 | 250,000-499,999 | 500,000-749,999 | 750,000-999,999 | 1,000,000+ |
|---|---|---|---|---|---|
| Average attendance | 150 | 313 | 483 | 665 | 1,247 |
| Average church income | 136,329 | 345,678 | 600,471 | 848,291 | 1,918,213 |
| Average years employed | 7 | 9 | 9 | 9 | 12 |
| Average compensation* | 43,457 | 54,482 | 65,066 | 68,584 | 85,531 |
| Standard deviation | 19,488 | 14,746 | 21,615 | 19,825 | 38,439 |

National average for all senior pastors: $56,172 with a standard deviation of $23,705 (see Chapter 4, Table 4-3).

Total respondents: 1,351

* includes base salary, housing or parsonage allowance, retirement contribution, life and health insurance payments, and educational funds (note: auto allowance is included in base salary).

## Table 5-3: Annual Compensation Of Senior Pastor By Church Setting And Size

| Attendance 0-250 | Urban | Suburban | Medium City | Small Town | Rural |
|---|---|---|---|---|---|
| Number Of Respondents | 87 | 205 | 140 | 248 | 89 |
| Salary (99%*) | 28,002 | 28,487 | 27,032 | 25,741 | 21,907 |
| Annual % Increase (65%) | 6% | 6% | 6% | 5% | 5% |
| Parsonage (20%) | 11,817 | 14,384 | 8,258 | 6,429 | 6,881 |
| Housing (81%) | 14,643 | 16,130 | 13,860 | 11,913 | 10,289 |
| Retirement (70%) | 4,184 | 4,163 | 3,958 | 3,459 | 3,395 |
| Life Insurance (31%) | 2,099 | 1,521 | 1,761 | 1,053 | 1,088 |
| Health Insurance (77%) | 4,731 | 5,042 | 4,528 | 4,187 | 4,339 |
| Vacation/weeks (95%) | 3 | 3 | 3 | 3 | 3 |
| Education Funds (44%) | 1,085 | 1,133 | 1,122 | 986 | 633 |
| Receive Auto Allow.(68%) | 64% | 70% | 59% | 49% | 52% |

* The percentage following each compensation item indicates the portion of all senior pastors who received that form of compensation. The averages in each column are for those individuals who actually received that compensation item. Auto allowance is included as part of base salary. See Chapter for a full explanation of how to read this table.

## Total Compensation Comparisons

| Church Size: 0-250 | Urban | Suburban | Medium City | Small Town | Rural |
|---|---|---|---|---|---|
| Average attendance | 140 | 155 | 152 | 142 | 136 |
| Average church income | 302,187 | 216,459 | 196,500 | 159,736 | 144,899 |
| Average years employed | 9 | 7 | 9 | 7 | 7 |
| Average compensation* | 48,865 | 52,397 | 46,945 | 42,053 | 37,665 |
| Standard deviation | 17,211 | 19,858 | 15,411 | 21,667 | 13,534 |

National average for all senior pastors: $56,172 with a standard deviation of $23,705 (see Chapter 4, Table 4-3).

Total respondents:769

* includes base salary, housing or parsonage allowance, retirement contribution, life and health insurance payments, and educational funds (note: auto allowance is included in base salary).

## Table 5-4: Annual Compensation Of Senior Pastor By Church Setting And Size

| Attendance 251-500 | Urban | Suburban | Medium City | Small Town | Rural |
|---|---|---|---|---|---|
| Number Of Respondents | 34 | 147 | 92 | 81 | 11 |
| Salary (99%*) | 41,247 | 32,999 | 33,628 | 31,529 | 34,365 |
| Annual % Increase (65%) | 4% | 5% | 4% | 5% | 4% |
| Parsonage (20%) | 23,365 | 14,119 | 14,636 | 21,868 | 4,733 |
| Housing (81%) | 23,119 | 20,807 | 15,603 | 15,210 | 7,702 |
| Retirement (70%) | 5,289 | 4,485 | 4,448 | 4,300 | 2,226 |
| Life Insurance (31%) | 653 | 1,063 | 781 | 1,124 | 354 |
| Health Insurance (77%) | 5,110 | 5,347 | 5,338 | 4,943 | 5,195 |
| Vacation/weeks (95%) | 4 | 4 | 4 | 3 | 3 |
| Education Funds (44%) | 1,920 | 1,216 | 1,416 | 1,052 | 670 |
| Receive Auto Allow.(68%) | 59% | 73% | 74.% | 75% | 73% |

* The percentage following each compensation item indicates the portion of all senior pastors who received that form of compensation. The averages in each column are for those individuals who actually received that compensation item. Auto allowance is included as part of base salary. See Chapter for a full explanation of how to read this table.

## Total Compensation Comparisons

| Church Size: 251-500 | Urban | Suburban | Medium City | Small Town | Rural |
|---|---|---|---|---|---|
| Average attendance | 378 | 368 | 370 | 368 | 338 |
| Average church income | 698,662 | 545,716 | 441,641 | 392,662 | 287,842 |
| Average years employed | 7 | 9 | 7 | 9 | 7 |
| Average compensation* | 68,848 | 61,267 | 57,011 | 54,131 | 45,341 |
| Standard deviation | 38,194 | 15,805 | 18,278 | 25,665 | 15,947 |

National average for all senior pastors: $56,172 with a standard deviation of $23,705 (see Chapter 4, Table 4-3).

Total respondents: 365

* includes base salary, housing or parsonage allowance, retirement contribution, life and health insurance payments, and educational funds (note: auto allowance is included in base salary).

## Table 5-5: Annual Compensation Of Senior Pastor By Church Setting And Size

| Attendance 501-750 | Urban | Suburban | Medium City | Small Town | Rural |
|---|---|---|---|---|---|
| Number Of Respondents | 25 | 48 | 48 | 23 | 0 |
| Salary (99%*) | 39,860 | 38,763 | 39,453 | 37,442 | |
| Annual % Increase (65%) | 6% | 5% | 5% | 7% | |
| Parsonage (20%) | 15,700 | 16,204 | 16,000 | 7,300 | |
| Housing (81%) | 21,359 | 19,993 | 18,873 | 19,517 | |
| Retirement (70%) | 4,368 | 4,893 | 5,239 | 4,074 | |
| Life Insurance (31%) | 1,333 | 935 | 1,400 | 445 | |
| Health Insurance (77%) | 5,660 | 5,103 | 5,404 | 4,462 | |
| Vacation/weeks (95%) | 4 | 4 | 4 | 4 | |
| Education Funds (44%) | 1,091 | 1,524 | 1,275 | 1,146 | |
| Receive Auto Allow.(68%) | 84% | 85% | 81% | 78% | |

* The percentage following each compensation item indicates the portion of all senior pastors who received that form of compensation. The averages in each column are for those individuals who actually received that compensation item. Auto allowance is included as part of base salary. See Chapter for a full explanation of how to read this table.

## Total Compensation Comparisons

| Church Size: 501-750 | Urban | Suburban | Medium City | Small Town | Rural |
|---|---|---|---|---|---|
| Average attendance | 624 | 628 | 620 | 627 | |
| Average church income | 938,655 | 829,068 | 792,172 | 837,367 | |
| Average years employed | 8 | 11 | 9 | 10 | |
| Average compensation* | 69,469 | 68,210 | 67,093 | 64,923 | |
| Standard deviation | 17,150 | 18,260 | 15,960 | 18,453 | |

National average for all senior pastors: $56,172 with a standard deviation of $23,705 (see Chapter 4, Table 4-3).

Total respondents: 144

* includes base salary, housing or parsonage allowance, retirement contribution, life and health insurance payments, and educational funds (note: auto allowance is included in base salary).

## Table 5-6: Annual Compensation Of Senior Pastor By Church Setting And Size

| Attendance 751-1,000 | Urban | Suburban | Medium City | Small Town | Rural |
|---|---|---|---|---|---|
| Number Of Respondents | 13 | 36 | 26 | 8 | 0 |
| Salary (99%*) | 46,724 | 48,531 | 42,907 | 49,388 | |
| Annual % Increase (65%) | 5% | 6% | 5% | 4% | |
| Parsonage (20%) | 13,800 | 7,950 | 12,350 | 17,088 | |
| Housing (81%) | 22,358 | 22,421 | 21,414 | 21,543 | |
| Retirement (70%) | 5,879 | 6,003 | 4,043 | 4,698 | |
| Life Insurance (31%) | 680 | 950 | 993 | 96 | |
| Health Insurance (77%) | 4,421 | 6,095 | 5,316 | 3,944 | |
| Vacation/weeks (95%) | 4 | 4 | 4 | 3 | |
| Education Funds (44%) | 1,033 | 1,131 | 1,146 | 3,067 | |
| Receive Auto Allow.(68%) | 77% | 89% | 77% | 75% | |

* The percentage following each compensation item indicates the portion of all senior pastors who received that form of compensation. The averages in each column are for those individuals who actually received that compensation item. Auto allowance is included as part of base salary. See Chapter for a full explanation of how to read this table.

## Total Compensation Comparisons

| Church Size: 751-1000 | Urban | Suburban | Medium Town | Small Town | Rural |
|---|---|---|---|---|---|
| Average attendance | 844 | 894 | 900 | 850 | |
| Average church income | 1,189,653 | 1,322,541 | 1,063,990 | 1,285,472 | |
| Average years employed | 10 | 11 | 11 | 13 | |
| Average compensation* | 74,678 | 79,624 | 71,563 | 77,954 | |
| Standard deviation | 24,388 | 20,156 | 14,728 | 12,947 | |

National average for all senior pastors: $56,172 with a standard deviation of $23,705 (see Chapter 4, Table 4-3).

Total respondents: 83

* includes base salary, housing or parsonage allowance, retirement contribution, life and health insurance payments, and educational funds (note: auto allowance is included in base salary).

## Table 5-7: Annual Compensation Of Senior Pastor By Church Setting And Size

| Attendance Over 1,000 | Urban | Suburban | Medium City | Small Town | Rural |
|---|---|---|---|---|---|
| Number Of Respondents | 11 | 67 | 28 | 8 | 2 |
| Salary (99%*) | 60,913 | 55,089 | 44,421 | 40,220 | 38,420 |
| Annual % Increase (65%) | 4% | 5% | 6% | 5% | 8% |
| Parsonage (20%) | 19,400 | 15,860 | 27,000 | 0 | 0 |
| Housing (81%) | 29,965 | 29,640 | 23,151 | 14,993 | 20,000 |
| Retirement (70%) | 11,338 | 7,212 | 4,613 | 3,684 | 7,305 |
| Life Insurance (31%) | 1,261 | 1,657 | 499 | 460 | 1,108 |
| Health Insurance (77%) | 5,149 | 5,963 | 4,599 | 4,815 | 5,494 |
| Vacation/weeks (95%) | 4 | 4 | 4 | 3 | 4 |
| Education Funds (44%) | 4,617 | 2,180 | 1,983 | 875 | 1,000 |
| Receive Auto Allow.(68%) | 100% | 78% | 89% | 88% | 100% |

\* The percentage following each compensation item indicates the portion of all senior pastors who received that form of compensation. The averages in each column are for those individuals who actually received that compensation item. Auto allowance is included as part of base salary. See Chapter for a full explanation of how to read this table.

## Total Compensation Comparisons

| Church Size: 1,000 + | Urban | Suburban | Medium City | Small Town | Rural |
|---|---|---|---|---|---|
| Average attendance | 1,855 | 1,802 | 1,572 | 1,906 | 1,100 |
| Average church income | 2,804,825 | 2,511,262 | 1,688,593 | 1,215,013 | 1,254,500 |
| Average years employed | 13 | 14 | 12 | 11 | 8 |
| Average compensation* | 102,606 | 94,732 | 73,310 | 59,759 | 72,772 |
| Standard deviation | 52,490 | 54,429 | 25,778 | 19,394 | 2,116 |

National average for all senior pastors: $56,172 with a standard deviation of $23,705 (see Chapter 4, Table 4-3).

Total respondents: 116

\* includes base salary, housing or parsonage allowance, retirement contribution, life and health insurance payments, and educational funds (note: auto allowance is included in base salary).

### Table 5-8: Annual Compensation Of Senior Pastor By Gender

| Gender | Male | Female |
|---|---|---|
| Number Of Respondents | 1,466 | 33 |
| Salary (99%*) | 32,588 | 32,649 |
| Annual % Increase (65%) | 5% | 4% |
| Parsonage (20%) | 11,348 | 9,479 |
| Housing (81%) | 17,058 | 12,077 |
| Retirement (70%) | 4,442 | 3,782 |
| Life Insurance (31%) | 1,163 | 1,336 |
| Health Insurance (77%) | 4,995 | 3,206 |
| Vacation/weeks (95%) | 3 | 4 |
| Education Funds (44%) | 1,249 | 992 |
| Receive Auto Allow.(68%) | 68% | 52% |

* The percentage following each compensation item indicates the portion of all senior pastors who received that form of compensation. The averages in each column are for those individuals who actually received that compensation item. Auto allowance is included as part of base salary. See Chapter  for a full explanation of how to read this table.

### Total Compensation Comparisons

| Gender | Male | Female |
|---|---|---|
| Average attendance | 427 | 193 |
| Average church income | 566,080 | 366,925 |
| Average years employed | 9 | 5 |
| Average compensation* | 56,431 | 46,269 |
| Standard deviation | 26,698 | 21,282 |

National average for all senior pastors: $56,172 with a standard deviation of $23,705 (see Chapter 4, Table 4-3).

Total respondents: 1,499

* includes base salary, housing or parsonage allowance, retirement contribution, life and health insurance payments, and educational funds (note: auto allowance is included in base salary).

## Table 5-9: Annual Compensation Of Senior Pastor By Education

| Highest Degree | High School | Associate | Bachelor | Master | Doctorate |
|---|---|---|---|---|---|
| Number Of Respondents | 50 | 54 | 363 | 556 | 313 |
| Salary (99%%*) | 27,335 | 25,975 | 28,810 | 32,963 | 39,421 |
| Annual % Increase (65%) | 8% | 5% | 6% | 5% | 5% |
| Parsonage (20%) | 7,800 | 8,000 | 10,220 | 10,848 | 14,581 |
| Housing (81%) | 12,932 | 14,065 | 15,715 | 17,163 | 19,406 |
| Retirement (70%) | 2,798 | 3,295 | 3,238 | 4,320 | 5,938 |
| Life Insurance (31%) | 507 | 552 | 1,273 | 914 | 1,430 |
| Health Insurance (77%) | 3,640 | 3,850 | 4,758 | 4,915 | 5,667 |
| Vacation/weeks (95%) | 3 | 3 | 3 | 4 | 4 |
| Education Funds (44%) | 1,017 | 979 | 991 | 1,190 | 1,549 |
| Receive Auto Allow.(68%) | 58% | 67% | 64% | 69% | 76% |

* The percentage following each compensation item indicates the portion of all senior pastors who received that form of compensation. The averages in each column are for those individuals who actually received that compensation item. Auto allowance is included as part of base salary. See Chapter for a full explanation of how to read this table.

## Total Compensation Comparisons

| Highest Degree | High School | Associate | Bachelor | Masters | Doctorate |
|---|---|---|---|---|---|
| Average attendance | 297 | 253 | 363 | 398 | 605 |
| Average church income | 302,049 | 316,061 | 460,696 | 487,431 | 927,030 |
| Average years employed | 10 | 8 | 9 | 8 | 9 |
| Average compensation* | 43,561 | 45,417 | 50,076 | 56,798 | 68,552 |
| Standard deviation | 20,907 | 14,203 | 20,390 | 27,039 | 30,111 |

National average for all senior pastors: $56,172 with a standard deviation of $23,705 (see Chapter 4, Table 4-3).

Total respondents: 1,336

* includes base salary, housing or parsonage allowance, retirement contribution, life and health insurance payments, and educational funds (note: auto allowance is included in base salary).

## Table 5-10: Annual Compensation Of Senior Pastor By Years Employed

| Years Employed | 0-5 | 6-10 | 11-15 | over 15 |
|---|---|---|---|---|
| Number Of Respondents | 661 | 381 | 184 | 234 |
| Salary (99%%*) | 29,958 | 32,999 | 32,756 | 38,777 |
| Annual % Increase (65%) | 6% | 5% | 5% | 5% |
| Parsonage (20%) | 10,567 | 13,781 | 12,582 | 10,476 |
| Housing (81%) | 15,703 | 17,927 | 17,426 | 18,474 |
| Retirement (70%) | 4,011 | 4,289 | 4,428 | 5,588 |
| Life Insurance (31%) | 1,173 | 1,100 | 1,281 | 1,277 |
| Health Insurance (77%) | 4,632 | 5,031 | 5,093 | 5,491 |
| Vacation/weeks (95%) | 3 | 3 | 4 | 4 |
| Education Funds (44%) | 1,144 | 1,250 | 1,414 | 1,408 |
| Receive Auto Allow.(68%) | 63% | 72% | 73% | 74% |

* The percentage following each compensation item indicates the portion of all senior pastors who received that form of compensation. The averages in each column are for those individuals who actually received that compensation item. Auto allowance is included as part of base salary. See Chapter for a full explanation of how to read this table.

## Total Compensation Comparisons

| Years Employed | 0-5 | 6-10 | 11-15 | Over 15 |
|---|---|---|---|---|
| Average attendance | 341 | 396 | 526 | 614 |
| Average church income | 440,481 | 562,304 | 594,639 | 882,236 |
| Average years employed | 3 | 8 | 13 | 22 |
| Average compensation* | 51,387 | 57,910 | 57,486 | 66,023 |
| Standard deviation | 22,112 | 30,709 | 23,536 | 30,791 |

National average for all senior pastors: $56,172 with a standard deviation of $23,705 (see Chapter 4, Table 4-3).

Total respondents: 1,460

* includes base salary, housing or parsonage allowance, retirement contribution, life and health insurance payments, and educational funds (note: auto allowance is included in base salary).

## Table 5-11: Annual Compensation Of Part-Time Senior Pastors By Hours Worked

| Hours Per Week | 1-14 | 15-29 | 30-39 | All Part-time |
|---|---|---|---|---|
| Number of Respondents | 0 | 12 | 9 | 44** |
| Salary (82%*) | | 9,047 | 20,008 | 15,644 |
| Annual % Increase (36%) | | 8% | 8% | 7% |
| Parsonage (23%) | | 5,900 | 7,200 | 7,424 |
| Housing (52%) | | 12,092 | 6,675 | 9,032 |
| Retirement (32%) | | 1,191 | 2,620 | 3,203 |
| Life Insurance (11%) | | 225 | 355 | 469 |
| Health Insurance (23%) | | 3,616 | 3,823 | 3,667 |
| Vacation/weeks (70%) | | 3 | 3 | 3 |
| Education Funds (27%) | | 638 | 350 | 554 |
| Receive Auto Allow. (61%) | | 92% | 89% | 61% |

* The percentage following each compensation item indicates the portion of all part-time senior pastors who received that form of compensation. The averages in each column are for those individuals who actually received that compensation item. Auto allowance is included as part of base salary. See Chapter for a full explanation of how to read this table.

** Some respondents did not indicate the number of hours worked.

## Total Compensation Comparisons

| Hours Per Week | 1-14 | 15-29 | 30-39 | All Part-time |
|---|---|---|---|---|
| Average attendance | | 140 | 114 | 126 |
| Average church income | | 148,321 | 121,111 | 132,050 |
| Average years employed | | 6 | 6 | 6 |
| Average hours per week | | 21 | 31 | 25 |
| Average compensation | | 17,616 | 28,349 | 22,278 |
| Ave. hourly compensation* | | 16.13 | 17.59 | 17.14 |
| Ave. hourly salary** | | 8.28 | 12.41 | 12.03 |

Total respondents: 447

* includes base salary, housing or parsonage allowance, retirement contribution, life and health insurance payments, and educational funds (note: auto allowance is included in base salary).

** includes base salary and auto allowance only; see discussion on "rounding errors" in Chapter 3.

# Chapter 6

# *Associate Pastors*

## Employment Profile

The roles and duties of the associate pastor are quite diverse depending upon the church. Associate pastors receive approximately the same benefits as senior pastors, but the total compensation amounts are considerably less. In general, associate pastors tend to receive a compensation of about 80% of that of pastors. The gap widens even more once church attendance exceeds 1,000 or church income passes $1,000,000. The statistical profile of associate pastors was as follows:

|  | Full-time | Part-time |
|---|---|---|
| Number of Respondents | 591 | 110 |
| Ordained | 91% | 81% |
| Male | 90% | 81% |
| Female | 10% | 19% |
| Years employed | 6 | 5 |
| Self-employed | 6% | 10% |
| Church Employee | 94% | 90% |
| High School Diploma | 5% | 14% |
| Associate Degree | 6% | 4% |
| Bachelor Degree | 33% | 37% |
| Master Degree | 45% | 37% |
| Doctorate | 11% | 8% |

## Compensation Analysis

The analysis below is based upon the tables found later in this chapter. The tables present compensation data for associate pastors who serve full-time according to worship attendance, church income, combinations of size and setting, gender, education, and years employed. The final table provides data for part-time pastors based upon the number of hours worked. In this way, the associate pastor's compensation can be analyzed and compared from a variety of useful perspectives. The total compensation amount was calculated by adding the base salary (plus auto allowance), housing or parsonage allowance, retirement contribution, life and health insurance payments, and educational funds.

# Key Points

✎ *Church worship attendance had a direct influence upon the compensation of the associate pastor.* Associate pastors in churches with an average attendance under 500 were below the national average; others were above. The value of several fringe benefits also tended to increase with church size. *See Table 6-1.*

✎ *Church income impacted the compensation of associate pastors.* Church income is the most important factor affecting total compensation, although many factors play a role. About 40% of the associate pastors served in churches with an average annual budget under $370,000. Housing allowance amount was closely associated with church income. Total compensation did not reach the national average until the church's annual income reached approached $600,000 per year. *See Table 6-2.*

✎ *A church's geographic setting impacted the compensation of associate pastors.* In general, associate pastors serving churches located in suburban, urban and medium size cities received the highest average compensation. Generally, urban churches tended to have the highest church income. Individuals serving in rural churches received the lowest average compensation. *See Tables 6-3, 6-4, 6-5, 6-6, and 6-7.*

✎ *Female associate pastors received lower levels of compensation than did their male counterparts.* The difference in total compensation was over $7,500 in 1997, up from $4,000 in 1996 and 7,000 in 1995. Men tended to serve in much larger churches with a budget averaging more than $300,000 more than those churches in which females served. That church income difference may account for a significant part of the compensation differential. *See Table 6-8.*

✎ *College graduates earned significantly more than nongraduates with those had obtained either a master's or doctoral degree.* Fifty-seven percent of this sample had graduate degrees. These individuals received higher levels of compensations than those with less education. They tended to work in urban or suburban churches which generally had significantly higher income than other churches. Associate pastors with a bachelor's degree earned 20% more than those with a high school diploma. Both, however, were below the national average. *See Table 6-9.*

✎ *Total compensation was partially tied to length of service.* Compensation increased with length of service. Those serving the longest tended to serve in churches with average annual incomes over $2,000,000. Church income is more significant than years served on final compensation amounts. *See Table 6-10.*

✎ *Most part-time associate pastors work about half-time at the church.* The average annual compensation for these part-time associates is about one-third of their full-time counterparts. *See Table 6-11.*

# Benefit Analysis

**Full-time staff members.** Full-time associate pastors received benefit packages commensurate with those of senior pastors. Senior pastors were more likely to live in a church owned parsonage than were associates, although a higher percentage of associates had a housing allowance as part of their compensation.

**Part-time staff members.** Over 15% percent of the associate pastors participating in this survey worked at their church on a part-time basis. Salary and benefits were tied to the number of hours employed.

| Benefits | Full-time | Part-time |
|---|---|---|
| ☐ Housing allowance | 86% | 40% |
| ☐ Parsonage provided | 9% | 4% |
| ☐ Retirement contributions | 63% | 19% |
| ☐ Life insurance | 30% | 9% |
| ☐ Health insurance | 79% | 20 % |
| ☐ Paid vacation | 94% | 49% |
| ☐ Auto allowance | 74% | 61% |
| ☐ Continuing education funds | 45% | 24% |

# Five Year Compensation Trend: National Averages for Associate Pastors

| | |
|---|---|
| ☐ 1993 | $39,970 |
| ☐ 1994 | $41,109 |
| ☐ 1995 | $44,058 |
| ☐ 1996 | $44,710 |
| ☐ 1997 | $45,042 |

## Table 6-1: Annual Compensation Of Associate Pastor By Worship Attendance

| Church Attendance | 0-99 | 100-299 | 300-499 | 500-749 | 750-999 | 1,000+ |
|---|---|---|---|---|---|---|
| Number Of Respondents | 5 | 124 | 142 | 120 | 65 | 112 |
| Salary (99%*) | 11,960 | 18,384 | 23,426 | 26,094 | 26,451 | 30,467 |
| Annual % Increase (68%) | 6% | 6% | 5% | 5% | 5% | 4% |
| Parsonage (9%) | 0 | 8,965 | 8,006 | 10,958 | 5,400 | 13,471 |
| Housing (86%) | 9,196 | 12,172 | 14,767 | 16,753 | 16,861 | 18,595 |
| Retirement (63%) | 0 | 3,414 | 3,342 | 3,665 | 3,310 | 4,076 |
| Life Insurance (30%) | 0 | 647 | 942 | 651 | 465 | 796 |
| Health Insurance (79%) | 3,210 | 3,630 | 4,782 | 4,634 | 5,100 | 4,979 |
| Vacation/weeks (94%) | 2 | 3 | 3 | 3 | 3 | 3 |
| Education Funds (45%) | 0 | 732 | 967 | 1,123 | 1,059 | 1,191 |
| Receive Auto Allow.(74%) | 60% | 63% | 71% | 77% | 83% | 80% |

* The percentage following each compensation item indicates the portion of all senior pastors who received that form of compensation. The averages in each column are for those individuals who actually received that compensation item. Auto allowance is included as part of base salary. See Chapter for a full explanation of how to read this table.

## Total Compensation Comparisons

| Church Attendance | 0-99 | 100-299 | 300-499 | 500-749 | 750-999 | Over 1,000 |
|---|---|---|---|---|---|---|
| Average attendance | 78 | 212 | 376 | 592 | 841 | 1,710 |
| Average church income | 114,875 | 274,190 | 505,728 | 869,359 | 1,179,920 | 2,188,838 |
| Average years employed | 1 | 4 | 5 | 7 | 7 | 9 |
| Annual compensation* | 20,579 | 33,578 | 42,997 | 49,147 | 49,682 | 54,353 |
| Standard deviation | 8,326 | 13,001 | 14,358 | 11,816 | 12,046 | 18,811 |

National average for all assoc. pastors: $45,042 with a standard deviation of $16,134 (see Chapter 4, Table 4-3).

Total respondents: 568

* includes base salary, housing or parsonage allowance, retirement contribution, life and health insurance payments, and educational funds (note: auto allowance is included in base salary).

## Table 6-2: Annual Compensation Of Associate Pastor By Church Income

| Church Income in $ | 0-249,999 | 250,000-499,999 | 500,000-749,000 | 750,000-999,999 | 1,000,000 + |
|---|---|---|---|---|---|
| Number Of Respondents | 71 | 141 | 89 | 61 | 170 |
| Salary (99%*) | 16,819 | 20,609 | 26,165 | 26,389 | 29,986 |
| Annual % Increase (68%) | 6% | 5% | 5% | 4% | 4% |
| Parsonage (9%) | 6,270 | 8,150 | 10,956 | 15,812 | 11,888 |
| Housing (86%) | 10,382 | 14,851 | 13,862 | 17,849 | 18,477 |
| Retirement (63%) | 1,887 | 3,627 | 3,469 | 3,609 | 4,126 |
| Life Insurance (30%) | 800 | 788 | 774 | 844 | 691 |
| Health Insurance (79%) | 2,870 | 4,276 | 4,728 | 5,061 | 5,090 |
| Vacation/weeks (94%) | 3 | 3 | 3 | 3 | 4 |
| Education Funds (45%) | 619 | 987 | 907 | 1,069 | 1,160 |
| Receive Auto Allow.(74%) | 58% | 65% | 72% | 75% | 83% |

* The percentage following each compensation item indicates the portion of all senior pastors who received that form of compensation. The averages in each column are for those individuals who actually received that compensation item. Auto allowance is included as part of base salary. See Chapter for a full explanation of how to read this table.

## Total Compensation Comparisons

| Church Budget | 0-249,999 | 250,000-499,999 | 500,000-749,999 | 750,000-999,999 | Over 1,000,000 |
|---|---|---|---|---|---|
| Average attendance | 229 | 347 | 516 | 703 | 1,328 |
| Average church income | 170,659 | 370,176 | 595,504 | 854,030 | 1,990,070 |
| Average years employed | 3 | 5 | 6 | 6 | 8 |
| Annual compensation* | 27,864 | 39,686 | 45,460 | 50,734 | 54,944 |
| Standard deviation | 10,361 | 12,644 | 10,796 | 14,425 | 16,638 |

National average for all assoc. pastors: $45,042 with a standard deviation of $16,134 (see Chapter 4, Table 4-3).

Total respondents: 532

* includes base salary, housing or parsonage allowance, retirement contribution, life and health insurance payments, and educational funds (note: auto allowance is included in base salary).

## Table 6-3: Annual Compensation Of Associate Pastor By Church Setting And Size

| Attendance 0-250 | Urban | Suburban | Medium City | Small Town | Rural |
|---|---|---|---|---|---|
| Number Of Respondents | 16 | 31 | 30 | 32 | 8 |
| Salary (99%*) | 22,746 | 18,898 | 20,560 | 17,228 | 15,578 |
| Annual % Increase (68%) | 8% | 5% | 5% | 5% | 8% |
| Parsonage (9%) | 0 | 12,596 | 11,300 | 4,981 | 4,543 |
| Housing (86%) | 17,274 | 14,634 | 10,621 | 11,130 | 10,600 |
| Retirement (63%) | 2,763 | 3,259 | 2,221 | 1,945 | 2,191 |
| Life Insurance (30%) | 210 | 439 | 687 | 330 | 246 |
| Health Insurance (79%) | 3,906 | 4,414 | 3,841 | 2,746 | 3,980 |
| Vacation/weeks (94%) | 2 | 3 | 3 | 2 | 3 |
| Education Funds (45%) | 896 | 754 | 1,075 | 541 | 400 |
| Receive Auto Allow.(74%) | 88% | 68% | 63% | 44% | 50% |

\* The percentage following each compensation item indicates the portion of all senior pastors who received that form of compensation. The averages in each column are for those individuals who actually received that compensation item. Auto allowance is included as part of base salary. See Chapter for a full explanation of how to read this table.

## Total Compensation Comparisons

| Church Size: 0-250 | Urban | Suburban | Medium City | Small Town | Rural |
|---|---|---|---|---|---|
| Average attendance | 199 | 178 | 204 | 181 | 167 |
| Average church income | 649,826 | 356,617 | 289,077 | 213,770 | 189,099 |
| Average years employed | 4 | 4 | 4 | 4 | 4 |
| Annual compensation* | 36,607 | 37,717 | 34,674 | 28,948 | 31,766 |
| Standard deviation | 14,599 | 12,807 | 13,835 | 13,488 | 6,298 |

National average for all assoc. pastors: $45,042 with a standard deviation of $16,134 (see Chapter 4, Table 4-3).

Total respondents: 117

\* includes base salary, housing or parsonage allowance, retirement contribution, life and health insurance payments, and educational funds (note: auto allowance is included in base salary).

## Table 6-4: Annual Compensation Of Associate Pastor By Church Setting And Size

| Attendance 251-500 | Urban | Suburban | Medium City | Small Town | Rural |
|---|---|---|---|---|---|
| Number Of Respondents | 15 | 90 | 48 | 35 | 2 |
| Salary (99%*) | 32,636 | 24,086 | 21,856 | 19,417 | 15,088 |
| Annual % Increase (68%) | 5% | 5% | 5% | 4% | 0 |
| Parsonage (9%) | 6,000 | 11,325 | 8,616 | 5,263 | 3,950 |
| Housing (86%) | 18,447 | 16,219 | 13,856 | 12,572 | 700 |
| Retirement (63%) | 4,180 | 3,353 | 4,932 | 3,322 | 0 |
| Life Insurance (30%) | 946 | 906 | 705 | 1,109 | 0 |
| Health Insurance (79%) | 4,183 | 4,994 | 4,218 | 4,253 | 5,125 |
| Vacation/weeks (94%) | 3 | 3 | 3 | 3 | 2 |
| Education Funds (45%) | 925 | 849 | 1,260 | 895 | 0 |
| Receive Auto Allow.(74%) | 53% | 72% | 77% | 71% | 100% |

* The percentage following each compensation item indicates the portion of all senior pastors who received that form of compensation. The averages in each column are for those individuals who actually received that compensation item. Auto allowance is included as part of base salary. See Chapter for a full explanation of how to read this table.

## Total Compensation Comparisons

| Church Size: 251-500 | Urban | Suburban | Medium City | Small Town | Rural |
|---|---|---|---|---|---|
| Average attendance | 386 | 378 | 367 | 378 | 370 |
| Average church income | 811,107 | 544,328 | 451,313 | 374,568 | 318,206 |
| Average years employed | 4 | 6 | 5 | 5 | 2 |
| Annual compensation* | 51,058 | 46,411 | 40,984 | 36,546 | 21,950 |
| Standard deviation | 23,960 | 13,082 | 14,678 | 12,009 | 12,758 |

National average for all assoc. pastors: $45,042 with a standard deviation of $16,134 (see Chapter 4, Table 4-3).

Total respondents: 190

* includes base salary, housing or parsonage allowance, retirement contribution, life and health insurance payments, and educational funds (note: auto allowance is included in base salary).

## Table 6-5: Annual Compensation Of Associate Pastor By Church Setting And Size

| Attendance 501-750 | Urban | Suburban | Medium City | Small Town | Rural |
|---|---|---|---|---|---|
| Number Of Respondents | 20 | 35 | 39 | 16 | 0 |
| Salary (99%*) | 25,434 | 27,248 | 24,597 | 26,497 | |
| Annual % Increase (68%) | 4% | 5% | 5% | 6% | |
| Parsonage (9%) | 19,925 | 2,000 | 0 | 5,000 | |
| Housing (86%) | 16,060 | 16,278 | 16,560 | 13,893 | |
| Retirement (63%) | 3,746 | 3,789 | 3,540 | 2,336 | |
| Life Insurance (30%) | 202 | 403 | 1,218 | 211 | |
| Health Insurance (79%) | 4,877 | 4,830 | 4,549 | 4,397 | |
| Vacation/weeks (94%) | 4 | 3 | 3 | 3 | |
| Education Funds (45%) | 1,045 | 1,203 | 1,175 | 958 | |
| Receive Auto Allow.(74%) | 85% | 83% | 79% | 62% | |

* The percentage following each compensation item indicates the portion of all senior pastors who received that form of compensation. The averages in each column are for those individuals who actually received that compensation item. Auto allowance is included as part of base salary. See Chapter for a full explanation of how to read this table.

## Total Compensation Comparisons

| Church Size: 0501-750 | Urban | Suburban | Medium City | Small Town | Rural |
|---|---|---|---|---|---|
| Average attendance | 633 | 629 | 617 | 629 | |
| Average church income | 1,038,137 | 892,614 | 860,125 | 821,423 | |
| Average years employed | 6 | 7 | 8 | 7 | |
| Annual compensation* | 47,610 | 50,551 | 48,763 | 44,384 | |
| Standard deviation | 11,572 | 9,254 | 11,164 | 7,670 | |

National average for all assoc. pastors: $45,042 with a standard deviation of $16,134 (see Chapter 4, Table 4-3).

Total respondents: 110

* includes base salary, housing or parsonage allowance, retirement contribution, life and health insurance payments, and educational funds (note: auto allowance is included in base salary).

## Table 6-6: Annual Compensation Of Associate Pastor By Church Setting And Size

| Attendance 751-1,000 | Urban | Suburban | Medium City | Small Town | Rural |
|---|---|---|---|---|---|
| Number Of Respondents | 8 | 30 | 19 | 7 | 0 |
| Salary (99%*) | 26,138 | 27,351 | 26,157 | 27,214 | |
| Annual % Increase (68%) | 4% | 5% | 5% | 4% | |
| Parsonage (9%) | 0 | 2,400 | 8,400 | 0 | |
| Housing (86%) | 20,776 | 18,625 | 15,486 | 14,317 | |
| Retirement (63%) | 4,312 | 3,549 | 2,718 | 4,451 | |
| Life Insurance (30%) | 363 | 632 | 622 | 0 | |
| Health Insurance (79%) | 5,087 | 5,781 | 5,079 | 4,155 | |
| Vacation/weeks (94%) | 4 | 3 | 3 | 3 | |
| Education Funds (45%) | 770 | 754 | 789 | 550 | |
| Receive Auto Allow.(74%) | 88% | 87% | 68% | 71% | |

* The percentage following each compensation item indicates the portion of all senior pastors who received that form of compensation. The averages in each column are for those individuals who actually received that compensation item. Auto allowance is included as part of base salary. See Chapter  for a full explanation of how to read this table.

## Total Compensation Comparisons

| Church Size: 751-1000 | Urban | Suburban | Medium City | Small Town | Rural |
|---|---|---|---|---|---|
| Average attendance | 869 | 883 | 911 | 835 | |
| Average church income | 1,481,090 | 1,272,092 | 1,056,164 | 1,208,297 | |
| Average years employed | 10 | 6 | 7 | 7 | |
| Annual compensation* | 54,671 | 49,994 | 48,046 | 46,334 | |
| Standard deviation | 9,389 | 14,101 | 12,218 | 10,826 | |

National average for all assoc. pastors: $45,042 with a standard deviation of $16,134 (see Chapter 4, Table 4-3).

Total respondents: 64

* includes base salary, housing or parsonage allowance, retirement contribution, life and health insurance payments, and educational funds (note: auto allowance is included in base salary).

## Table 6-7: Annual Compensation Of Associate Pastor By Church Setting And Size

| Attendance Over 1,000 | Urban | Suburban | Medium City | Small Town | Rural |
|---|---|---|---|---|---|
| Number Of Respondents | 10 | 59 | 24 | 6 | 2 |
| Salary (99%*) | 33,742 | 31,308 | 30,349 | 24,911 | 31,450 |
| Annual % Increase (68%) | 5% | 4% | 5% | 3% | 8 |
| Parsonage (9%) | 11,250 | 13,400 | 18,200 | 0 | 0 |
| Housing (86%) | 23,617 | 19,902 | 16,142 | 12,040 | 10,000 |
| Retirement (63%) | 6,440 | 4,375 | 2,796 | 4,428 | 5,785 |
| Life Insurance (30%) | 787 | 1,219 | 259 | 246 | 544 |
| Health Insurance (79%) | 4,261 | 5,212 | 4,575 | 5,418 | 4,986 |
| Vacation/weeks (94%) | 3 | 4 | 3 | 3 | 4 |
| Education Funds (45%) | 1,660 | 1,091 | 1,396 | 875 | 1,000 |
| Receive Auto Allow.(74%) | 100% | 73% | 92% | 83% | 100% |

* The percentage following each compensation item indicates the portion of all senior pastors who received that form of compensation. The averages in each column are for those individuals who actually received that compensation item. Auto allowance is included as part of base salary. See Chapter for a full explanation of how to read this table.

## Total Compensation Comparisons

| Church Size: 1,000 + | Urban | Suburban | Medium City | Small Town | Rural |
|---|---|---|---|---|---|
| Average attendance | 1,800 | 1,847 | 1,606 | 2,133 | 1,100 |
| Average church income | 2,485,308 | 2,570,561 | 1,756,376 | 1,418,167 | 1,254,500 |
| Average years employed | 8 | 9 | 8 | 10 | 11 |
| Annual compensation* | 62,359 | 58,272 | 49,830 | 39,503 | 53,494 |
| Standard deviation | 14,063 | 20,358 | 16,308 | 14,667 | 4,472 |

National average for all assoc. pastors: $45,042 with a standard deviation of $16,134 (see Chapter 4, Table 4-3).

Total respondents: 101

* includes base salary, housing or parsonage allowance, retirement contribution, life and health insurance payments, and educational funds (note: auto allowance is included in base salary).

## Table 6-8: Annual Compensation Of Associate Pastor By Gender

| Gender | Male | Female |
|---|---|---|
| Number Of Respondents | 532 | 57 |
| Salary (99%*) | 24,779 | 21,830 |
| Annual % Increase (68%) | 5% | 5% |
| Parsonage (9%) | 9,820 | 8,139 |
| Housing (86%) | 15,803 | 13,620 |
| Retirement (63%) | 3,429 | 5,087 |
| Life Insurance (30%) | 748 | 736 |
| Health Insurance (79%) | 4,660 | 3,899 |
| Vacation/weeks (94%) | 3 | 4 |
| Education Funds (45%) | 1,044 | 886 |
| Receive Auto Allow.(74%) | 74% | 74% |

\* The percentage following each compensation item indicates the portion of all senior pastors who received that form of compensation. The averages in each column are for those individuals who actually received that compensation item. Auto allowance is included as part of base salary. See Chapter  for a full explanation of how to read this table.

## Total Compensation Comparisons

| Gender | Male | Female |
|---|---|---|
| Average attendance | 727 | 422 |
| Average church income | 984,023 | 680,927 |
| Average years employed | 6 | 4 |
| Annual compensation* | 45,777 | 38,242 |
| Standard deviation | 15,806 | 17,955 |

National average for all assoc. pastors: $45,042 with a standard deviation of $16,134 (see Chapter 4, Table 4-3).

Total respondents: 589

\* includes base salary, housing or parsonage allowance, retirement contribution, life and health insurance payments, and educational funds (note: auto allowance is included in base salary).

## Table 6-9: Annual Compensation Of Associate Pastor By Education

| Highest Degree | High School | Associate | Bachelor | Master | Doctorate |
|---|---|---|---|---|---|
| Number Of Respondents | 23 | 29 | 166 | 234 | 55 |
| Salary (99%*) | 20,829 | 18,583 | 22,416 | 25,787 | 33,486 |
| Annual % Increase (68%) | 7% | 4% | 5% | 5% | 5% |
| Parsonage (9%) | 10,000 | 6,205 | 10,528 | 9,323 | 13,500 |
| Housing (%) | 17,365 | 13,480 | 14,598 | 16,158 | 18,403 |
| Retirement (63%) | 2,060 | 2,293 | 3,112 | 3,798 | 4,764 |
| Life Insurance (30%) | 180 | 562 | 648 | 656 | 1,293 |
| Health Insurance (79%) | 2,969 | 4,293 | 4,389 | 4,735 | 5,538 |
| Vacation/weeks (94%) | 2 | 3 | 3 | 3 | 4 |
| Education Funds (45%) | 638 | 705 | 916 | 1,060 | 1,337 |
| Receive Auto Allow.(74%) | 74% | 79% | 72% | 77% | 82% |

* The percentage following each compensation item indicates the portion of all senior pastors who received that form of compensation. The averages in each column are for those individuals who actually received that compensation item. Auto allowance is included as part of base salary. See Chapter for a full explanation of how to read this table.

## Total Compensation Comparisons

| Highest Degree | High School | Associate | Bachelor | Masters | Doctorate |
|---|---|---|---|---|---|
| Average attendance | 487 | 416 | 663 | 738 | 920 |
| Average church income | 730,463 | 559,075 | 884,892 | 929,667 | 1,754,262 |
| Average years employed | 6 | 6 | 5 | 6 | 9 |
| Annual compensation* | 34,285 | 36,809 | 41,795 | 48,073 | 58,954 |
| Standard deviation | 23,984 | 13,160 | 14,612 | 13,401 | 18,679 |

National average for all assoc. pastors: $45,042 with a standard deviation of $16,134 (see Chapter 4, Table 4-3).

Total respondents: 507

* includes base salary, housing or parsonage allowance, retirement contribution, life and health insurance payments, and educational funds (note: auto allowance is included in base salary).

### Table 6-10: Annual Compensation Of Associate Pastor By Years Employed

| Years Employed | 0-5 | 6-10 | 11-15 | over 15 |
|---|---|---|---|---|
| Number Of Respondents | 342 | 126 | 60 | 37 |
| Salary (99%*) | 22,620 | 26,317 | 28,417 | 30,667 |
| Annual % Increase (68%) | 5% | 5% | 4% | 3% |
| Parsonage (9%) | 8,211 | 13,470 | 0 | 14,850 |
| Housing (86%) | 14,850 | 15,580 | 18,561 | 18,153 |
| Retirement (63%) | 3,473 | 3,300 | 4,173 | 4,166 |
| Life Insurance (30%) | 751 | 751 | 414 | 1,364 |
| Health Insurance (79%) | 4,335 | 5,091 | 4,770 | 4,837 |
| Vacation/weeks (94%) | 3 | 3 | 3 | 4 |
| Education Funds (45%) | 947 | 1,040 | 1,254 | 1,465 |
| Receive Auto Allow.(74%) | 74% | 75% | 70% | 78% |

* The percentage following each compensation item indicates the portion of all senior pastors who received that form of compensation. The averages in each column are for those individuals who actually received that compensation item. Auto allowance is included as part of base salary. See Chapter for a full explanation of how to read this table.

### Total Compensation Comparisons

| Years Employed | 0-5 | 6-10 | 11-15 | Over 15 |
|---|---|---|---|---|
| Average attendance | 626 | 744 | 777 | 1,206 |
| Average church income | 772,385 | 1,020,246 | 1,296,423 | 2,201,923 |
| Average years employed | 3 | 8 | 13 | 22 |
| Annual compensation* | 41,255 | 49,536 | 51,580 | 56,156 |
| Standard deviation | 15,697 | 12,984 | 16,708 | 16,831 |

National average for all assoc. pastors: $45,042 with a standard deviation of $16,134 (see Chapter 4, Table 4-3).

Total respondents: 565

* includes base salary, housing or parsonage allowance, retirement contribution, life and health insurance payments, and educational funds (note: auto allowance is included in base salary).

## Table 6-11: Annual Compensation Of Part-Time Associate Pastors By Hours Worked

| Hours Per Week | 1-14 | 15-29 | 30-39 | All Part-time |
|---|---|---|---|---|
| Number of Respondents | 14 | 30 | 6 | 110** |
| Salary (80%*) | 5,962 | 11,865 | 20,028 | 10,962 |
| Annual % Increase (35%) | 6% | 4% | 3% | 6% |
| Parsonage (4%) | 8,820 | 0 | 0 | 7,505 |
| Housing (40%) | 10,490 | 8,410 | 13,074 | 9,144 |
| Retirement (19%) | 1,597 | 1,830 | 1,142 | 2,067 |
| Life Insurance (9%) | 44 | 0 | 257 | 252 |
| Health Insurance (20%) | 1,187 | 2,531 | 2,021 | 2,947 |
| Vacation/weeks (49%) | 3 | 3 | 4 | 3 |
| Education Funds (24%) | 733 | 296 | 1,000 | 812 |
| Receive Auto Allow. (61%) | 86% | 77% | 100% | 61% |

* The percentage following each compensation item indicates the portion of all part-time senior pastors who received that form of compensation. The averages in each column are for those individuals who actually received that compensation item. Auto allowance is included as part of base salary. See Chapter  for a full explanation of how to read this table.

** Some respondents did not indicate the number of hours worked.

## Total Compensation Comparisons

| Hours Worked Per Week | 1-14 | 15-29 | 30-39 | All Part-time |
|---|---|---|---|---|
| Average attendance | 234 | 295 | 438 | 303 |
| Average church income | 246,410 | 373,931 | 423,826 | 365,770 |
| Average years employed | 5 | 5 | 4 | 5 |
| Average hours per week | 8 | 20 | 31 | 18 |
| Average compensation | 8,698 | 14,045 | 28,787 | 14,433 |
| Ave. hourly compensation* | 20.91 | 13.50 | 17.86 | 15.42 |
| Ave. hourly salary** | 14.33 | 11.41 | 12.42 | 11.71 |

* includes base salary, housing or parsonage allowance, retirement contribution, life and health insurance payments, and educational funds (note: auto allowance is included in base salary).

** includes base salary and auto allowance only; see discussion on "rounding errors" in Chapter 3.

# Chapter 7

# *Christian Education Directors*

## Employment Profile

A majority of the Christian Education Directors participating in this study serve as ordained ministers. The vast majority are college graduates, and over 50% have graduate degrees. Christian Education Directors reflected the following profile:

|  | Full-time | Part-time |
|---|---|---|
| ☐ Number of Respondents | 322 | 159 |
| ☐ Ordained | 62% | 15% |
| ☐ Average Years Employed | 6 | 4 |
| ☐ Male | 63% | 17% |
| ☐ Female | 37% | 83% |
| ☐ Self-employed | 2% | 5% |
| ☐ Church Employee | 98% | 95% |
| ☐ High School Diploma | 7% | 9% |
| ☐ Associate Degree | 3% | 3% |
| ☐ Bachelor Degree | 38% | 65% |
| ☐ Master Degree | 48% | 21% |
| ☐ Doctorate | 4% | 2% |

## Compensation Analysis

The analysis below is based upon the tables found later in this chapter. The tables present compensation data according to worship attendance, church income, combinations of size and setting, gender, education, and years employed for CE Directors who serve full-time. The final table provides data for part-time CE directors based upon the number of hours worked. In this way, the CE Director's compensation can be viewed from a variety of useful perspectives. The total compensation amount found in a separate box at the bottom of each page was calculated by adding the base salary (including auto allowance), housing or parsonage amount, life and health insurance payments, retirement contribution, and educational funds.

# Key Points

✎ **CE Directors and youth ministers follow an almost identical pattern with respect to attendance and compensation.** Most full-time CE Directors serve in churches with an attendance over 500, with more than one-fourth in congregations over 1,000. Overall compensation remains below the national average until a position is secured in one of these larger churches. *See Table 7-1.*

✎ **Both church income and size correlate with compensation.** Compensation increased directly with the size of the church budget. From the standpoint of compensation, CE Directors are aligned with youth ministers and church administrators. CE Directors start off with slightly higher compensation levels. Income increases the most rapid once the church budget exceeds $1,000,000 per year. *See Table 7-2.*

✎ **CE Directors who work in churches with an average attendance under 500 have an annual compensation below the national average regardless of church setting.** Most CE Directors work in larger suburban churches, while very few work in rural settings. Overall compensation was slightly higher in large suburban churches. *See Tables 7-3 and 7-4.*

✎ **Significant gender differences exists for CE Directors.** A disparity of over $14,500 in annual total compensation was reported with men receiving the larger amount. Women worked in slightly smaller churches with an average attendance 12% less than men. However, overall church income was over $350,000 less in those churches with female CE Directors. While salary amounts were similar, the women in this study received lower fringe benefits. The difference in overall compensation can be attributed to gender more than any other variable. *See Table 7-5.*

✎ **Educational achievement had a relationship to compensation.** Overall compensation increased steadily with education. Yet, even college graduates were still below the national average. Fifty-two percent of the full-time Christian education directors surveyed had either a master's degree or a doctorate. Those with doctoral degrees earned on average nearly $19,000 more than the typical CE DIrector. *See Table 7-6.*

✎ **Employment longevity did not affect overall compensation.** Surprisingly, compensation did not increase with years of service, except for those serving 15 or more years. What can be said is that for this sample, those CE Directors with the most years of service tended to work in congregations with the largest incomes, but many actually earned less than those with less years of service. Those with five or less years of service were below the national average. *See Table 7-7.*

✎ **Many CE Directors work part-time.** Hourly compensation varied with the number of hours worked. The typical part-time CE Director worked 19 hours per week, and had been in the church for about four years. Fairly high turnover exists. *See Table 7-8.*

# Benefit Analysis

**Full-time staff members.** Full-time Christian education directors received benefit packages comparable to those of other professional and ministerial staff members within the church. Yet, since fewer are ordained, a smaller percentage received parsonage and housing allowances compared to ministerial staff members. In general, the Christian education director's average benefits are slightly less than those of associate pastors.

**Part-time staff members.** Over 80% of part-time Christian education directors are female. Ninety-five percent of part-time directors are church employees. Smaller churches were more likely to employ part-time directors than were larger churches. Part-time Christian education directors received few benefits with the most common being an auto allowance and a two week paid vacation.

| Benefits | Full-time | Part-time |
|---|---|---|
| Housing allowance | 58% | 8% |
| Parsonage provided | 2% | 1% |
| Retirement | 57% | 5% |
| Life insurance | 29% | 2% |
| Health insurance | 72% | 13% |
| Paid vacation | 93% | 52% |
| Auto allowance | 75% | 53% |
| Continuing education funds | 46% | 23% |

# Five Year Compensation Trend: National Averages for Christian Education Directors

- 1993   $35,291
- 1994   $37,676
- 1995   $37,453
- 1996   $38,855
- 1997   $40,863

## Table 7-1: Annual Compensation Of CE Director By Worship Attendance

| Church Attendance | 0-99 | 100-299 | 300-499 | 500-749 | 750-999 | over 1000 |
|---|---|---|---|---|---|---|
| Number Of Respondents | 0 | 42 | 62 | 68 | 52 | 83 |
| Salary (98%*) | | 21,330 | 24,350 | 24,623 | 28,412 | 30,172 |
| Annual % Increase (68%) | | 5% | 4% | 6% | 5% | 5% |
| Parsonage (2%) | | 6,960 | 0 | 15,000 | 8,400 | 12,000 |
| Housing (58%) | | 12,234 | 15,365 | 15,548 | 15,681 | 19,310 |
| Retirement (57%) | | 2,782 | 2,718 | 2,926 | 2,812 | 3,455 |
| Life Insurance (29%) | | 423 | 187 | 618 | 269 | 316 |
| Health Insurance (72%) | | 3,969 | 4,637 | 3,958 | 4,732 | 4,413 |
| Vacation/weeks (93%) | | 2 | 3 | 3 | 3 | 3 |
| Education Funds (46%) | | 803 | 830 | 864 | 874 | 1,280 |
| Auto Allowance (75%) | | 55% | 63% | 82% | 85% | 81% |

* The percentage following each compensation item indicates the portion of church administrators who received that form of compensation. The averages in each column are for those individuals who actually received that compensation item. Auto allowance is included as part of base salary. See Chapter 3 for a full explanation of how to read this table.

## Total Compensation Comparisons

| Church Attendance | 0-99 | 100-299 | 300-499 | 500-749 | 750-999 | Over 1,000 |
|---|---|---|---|---|---|---|
| Average attendance | | 207 | 384 | 601 | 846 | 1,774 |
| Average church income | | 279,317 | 617,702 | 912,231 | 1,296,200 | 2,345,479 |
| Average years employed | | 5 | 7 | 5 | 5 | 7 |
| Average compensation* | | 30,928 | 35,890 | 40,613 | 42,451 | 50,178 |
| Standard deviation | | 11,246 | 16,104 | 12,128 | 13,631 | 15,893 |

National average for all CE Directors: $40,863 with a standard deviation of $15,408 (see Chapter 4, Table 4-3).

Total respondents: 307

* includes base salary, housing or parsonage allowance, retirement contribution, life and health insurance payments, and educational funds (note: auto allowance is included in base salary).

## Table 7-2: Annual Compensation Of CE Director By Church Budget

| Church Budget in $ | 0-249,999 | 250,000-499,999 | 500,000-749,000 | 750,000-999,999 | 1,000,000 + |
|---|---|---|---|---|---|
| Number Of Respondents | 18 | 53 | 47 | 32 | 144 |
| Salary (98%*) | 21,356 | 21,153 | 23,187 | 24,098 | 29,756 |
| Annual % Increase (68%) | 6% | 4% | 6% | 6% | 5% |
| Parsonage (2%) | 1,920 | 6,000 | 13,500 | 9,200 | 14,000 |
| Housing (58%) | 12,317 | 13,511 | 12,951 | 15,929 | 18,308 |
| Retirement (57%) | 2,447 | 2,411 | 2,870 | 2,683 | 3,402 |
| Life Insurance (29%) | 544 | 177 | 319 | 700 | 295 |
| Health Insurance (72%) | 2.927 | 4,399 | 3,552 | 4,588 | 4,400 |
| Vacation/weeks (93%) | 2 | 3 | 3 | 3 | 3 |
| Education Funds (46%) | 840 | 839 | 748 | 775 | 1,148 |
| Auto Allowance (75%) | 56% | 60% | 62% | 78% | 83% |

* The percentage following each compensation item indicates the portion of church administrators who received that form of compensation. The averages in each column are for those individuals who actually received that compensation item. Auto allowance is included as part of base salary. See Chapter 3 for a full explanation of how to read this table.

## Total Compensation Comparisons

| Church Budget | 0-249,999 | 250,000-499,999 | 500,000-749,999 | 750,000-999,999 | 1,000,000+ |
|---|---|---|---|---|---|
| Average attendance | 210 | 338 | 506 | 713 | 1,304 |
| Average church income | 161,972 | 353,393 | 609,839 | 862,602 | 1,962,607 |
| Average years employed | 4 | 6 | 6 | 5 | 6 |
| Average compensation* | 29,491 | 31,162 | 34,806 | 40,348 | 47,973 |
| Standard deviation | 15,063 | 11,853 | 11,009 | 13,393 | 15,040 |

National average for all CE Directors: $40,863 with a standard deviation of $15,408 (see Chapter 4, Table 4-3).

Total respondents: 294

* includes base salary, housing or parsonage allowance, retirement contribution, life and health insurance payments, and educational funds (note: auto allowance is included in base salary).

## Table 7-3: Annual Compensation Of CE Director By Church Setting And Size

| Attendance Under 500 | Urban | Suburban | Medium City | Small Town | Rural |
|---|---|---|---|---|---|
| Number Of Respondents | 13 | 34 | 25 | 26 | 5 |
| Salary (98%*) | 25,776 | 23,460 | 21,610 | 23,808 | 14,896 |
| Annual % Increase (68%) | 3% | 4% | 5% | 4% | 7% |
| Parsonage (2%) | 0 | 12,000 | 0 | 0 | 0 |
| Housing (58%) | 14,372 | 14,774 | 15,273 | 13,300 | 10,000 |
| Retirement (57%) | 2,251 | 2,477 | 3,164 | 3,073 | 2,369 |
| Life Insurance (29%) | 181 | 342 | 135 | 170 | 149 |
| Health Insurance (72%) | 3,506 | 4,842 | 5,024 | 4,090 | 2,271 |
| Vacation/weeks (93%) | 3 | 3 | 3 | 2 | 2 |
| Education Funds (46%) | 570 | 891 | 935 | 732 | 0 |
| Auto Allowance (75%) | 62% | 62% | 56% | 58% | 60% |

* The percentage following each compensation item indicates the portion of church administrators who received that form of compensation. The averages in each column are for those individuals who actually received that compensation item. Auto allowance is included as part of base salary. See Chapter 3 for a full explanation of how to read this table.

## Total Compensation Comparisons

| Church Size: Under 500 | Urban | Suburban | Medium City | Small Town | Rural |
|---|---|---|---|---|---|
| Average attendance | 358 | 308 | 334 | 284 | 245 |
| Average church income | 743,592 | 513,818 | 408,720 | 414,244 | 197,806 |
| Average years employed | 6 | 7 | 7 | 5 | 4 |
| Average compensation* | 33,719 | 37,212 | 33,566 | 31,556 | 25,236 |
| Standard deviation | 8,202 | 15,361 | 15,526 | 13,742 | 15,082 |

National average for all CE Directors: $40,863 with a standard deviation of $15,408 (see Chapter 4, Table 4-3).

Total respondents: 103

* includes base salary, housing or parsonage allowance, retirement contribution, life and health insurance payments, and educational funds (note: auto allowance is included in base salary).

## Table 7-4: Annual Compensation Of CE Director By Church Setting And Size

| Attendance Over 499 | Urban | Suburban | Medium City | Small Town | Rural |
|---|---|---|---|---|---|
| Number Of Respondents | 28 | 96 | 58 | 19 | 0 |
| Salary (98%*) | 30,379 | 27,903 | 27,108 | 26,207 | |
| Annual % Increase (68%) | 7% | 5% | 5% | 4% | |
| Parsonage (2%) | 10,000 | 14,500 | 0 | 8,400 | |
| Housing (58%) | 14,596 | 19,512 | 14,992 | 14,180 | |
| Retirement (57%) | 4,146 | 3,111 | 2,899 | 2,613 | |
| Life Insurance (29%) | 384 | 255 | 652 | 180 | |
| Health Insurance (72%) | 4,644 | 4,356 | 4,515 | 2,958 | |
| Vacation/weeks (93%) | 3 | 3 | 3 | 3 | |
| Education Funds (46%) | 1,089 | 988 | 1,151 | 860 | |
| Auto Allowance (75%) | 89% | 78% | 86% | 79% | |

* The percentage following each compensation item indicates the portion of church administrators who received that form of compensation. The averages in each column are for those individuals who actually received that compensation item. Auto allowance is included as part of base salary. See Chapter 3 for a full explanation of how to read this table.

## Total Compensation Comparisons

| Attendance Over 499 | Urban | Suburban | Medium City | Small Town | Rural |
|---|---|---|---|---|---|
| Average attendance | 946 | 1,351 | 1,010 | 823 | |
| Average church income | 1,498,219 | 1,962,627 | 1,245,117 | 1,101,216 | |
| Average years employed | 7 | 6 | 5 | 6 | |
| Average compensation* | 44,872 | 47,087 | 43,280 | 39,143 | |
| Standard deviation | 17,886 | 14,656 | 13,394 | 13,572 | |

National average for all CE Directors: $40,863 with a standard deviation of $15,408 (see Chapter 4, Table 4-3).

Total respondents: 201

* includes base salary, housing or parsonage allowance, retirement contribution, life and health insurance payments, and educational funds (note: auto allowance is included in base salary).

## Table 7-5: Annual Compensation Of CE Director By Gender

| Gender | Male | Female |
|---|---|---|
| Number Of Respondents | 201 | 120 |
| Salary (98%*) | 27,595 | 25,884 |
| Annual % Increase (68%) | 5% | 5% |
| Parsonage (2%) | 10,220 | 6,000 |
| Housing (58%) | 16,262 | 16,148 |
| Retirement (57%) | 3,088 | 2,885 |
| Life Insurance (29%) | 330 | 405 |
| Health Insurance (72%) | 4,763 | 3,191 |
| Vacation/weeks (93%) | 3 | 3 |
| Education Funds (46%) | 1,084 | 818 |
| Auto Allowance (75%) | 82% | 63% |

* The percentage following each compensation item indicates the portion of church administrators who received that form of compensation. The averages in each column are for those individuals who actually received that compensation item. Auto allowance is included as part of base salary. See Chapter 3 for a full explanation of how to read this table.

## Total Compensation Comparisons

| Gender | Male | Female |
|---|---|---|
| Average attendance | 901 | 799 |
| Average church income | 1,363,109 | 1,006,419 |
| Average years employed | 5 | 7 |
| Average compensation* | 47,047 | 32,537 |
| Standard deviation | 23,412 | 12,103 |

National average for all CE Directors: $40,863 with a standard deviation of $15,408 (see Chapter 4, Table 4-3).

Total respondents: 321

* includes base salary, housing or parsonage allowance, retirement contribution, life and health insurance payments, and educational funds (note: auto allowance is included in base salary).

## Table 7-6: Annual Compensation Of CE Director By Education

| Highest Degree | High School | Associate | Bachelor | Master | Doctorate |
|---|---|---|---|---|---|
| Number Of Respondents | 20 | 7 | 105 | 131 | 11 |
| Salary (98%*) | 20,774 | 22,160 | 24,677 | 28,842 | 30,947 |
| Annual % Increase (68%) | 6% | 4% | 5% | 4% | 4% |
| Parsonage (2%) | 0 | 0 | 13,500 | 6,580 | 14,000 |
| Housing (58%) | 13,410 | 14,370 | 14,851 | 17,255 | 19,568 |
| Retirement (57%) | 2,272 | 2,815 | 2,383 | 3,473 | 3,409 |
| Life Insurance (29%) | 192 | 613 | 341 | 402 | 235 |
| Health Insurance (72%) | 4,874 | 2,979 | 4,375 | 4,257 | 4,590 |
| Vacation/weeks (93%) | 2 | 3 | 3 | 3 | 3 |
| Education Funds (46%) | 769 | 1,567 | 859 | 1,037 | 1,450 |
| Auto Allowance (75%) | 70% | 57% | 69% | 83% | 91% |

* The percentage following each compensation item indicates the portion of church administrators who received that form of compensation. The averages in each column are for those individuals who actually received that compensation item. Auto allowance is included as part of base salary. See Chapter 3 for a full explanation of how to read this table.

## Total Compensation Comparisons

| Highest Degree | High School | Associate | Bachelor | Master | Doctorate |
|---|---|---|---|---|---|
| Average attendance | 540 | 574 | 839 | 930 | 1,578 |
| Average church income | 805,986 | 902,441 | 1,086,528 | 1,350,154 | 3,321,783 |
| Average years employed | 7 | 7 | 6 | 6 | 5 |
| Average compensation* | 25,584 | 35,065 | 36,820 | 46,770 | 59,954 |
| Standard deviation | 11,455 | 15,944 | 13,014 | 14,519 | 11,583 |

National average for all CE Directors: $40,863 with a standard deviation of $15,408 (see Chapter 4, Table 4-3).

Total respondents: 274

* includes base salary, housing or parsonage allowance, retirement contribution, life and health insurance payments, and educational funds (note: auto allowance is included in base salary).

## Table 7-7: Annual Compensation Of CE Director By Years Employed

| Years Employed | 0-5 | 6-10 | 11-15 | over 15 |
|---|---|---|---|---|
| Number Of Respondents | 194 | 57 | 31 | 20 |
| Salary (98%*) | 24,402 | 28,298 | 28,834 | 33,099 |
| Annual % Increase (68%) | 5% | 4% | 4% | 5% |
| Parsonage (2%) | 9,617 | 0 | 0 | 0 |
| Housing (58%) | 15,876 | 16,604 | 15,337 | 22,178 |
| Retirement (57%) | 2,919 | 2,956 | 2,796 | 3,610 |
| Life Insurance (29%) | 346 | 455 | 315 | 302 |
| Health Insurance (72%) | 4,197 | 4,167 | 5,297 | 4,556 |
| Vacation/weeks (93%) | 3 | 3 | 4 | 4 |
| Education Funds (46%) | 885 | 1,091 | 1,068 | 1,139 |
| Auto Allowance (75%) | 77% | 77% | 71% | 80% |

* The percentage following each compensation item indicates the portion of church administrators who received that form of compensation. The averages in each column are for those individuals who actually received that compensation item. Auto allowance is included as part of base salary. See Chapter 3 for a full explanation of how to read this table.

## Total Compensation Comparisons

| Years Employed | 0-5 | 6-10 | 11-15 | Over 15 |
|---|---|---|---|---|
| Average attendance | 797 | 1,066 | 866 | 1,169 |
| Average church income | 1,089,089 | 1,477,743 | 1,214,540 | 2,357,354 |
| Average years employed | 3 | 8 | 13 | 19 |
| Average compensation* | 40,040 | 42,286 | 39,772 | 49,383 |
| Standard deviation | 14,702 | 13,218 | 17,238 | 17,822 |

National average for all CE Directors: $40,863 with a standard deviation of $15,408 (see Chapter 4, Table 4-3).

Total respondents: 302

* includes base salary, housing or parsonage allowance, retirement contribution, life and health insurance payments, and educational funds (note: auto allowance is included in base salary).

## Table 7-8: Annual Compensation Of Part-Time CE Directors By Hours Worked

| Hours-per-week | 1-14 | 15-29 | 30-39 | All Part-time |
|---|---|---|---|---|
| Number Of Respondents | 21 | 26 | 15 | 159 |
| Salary (89.0*) | 7,058 | 12,629 | 18,783 | 11,424 |
| Annual % Increase (57%) | 4% | 6% | 4% | 6% |
| Parsonage (1%) | 12,000 | 0 | 0 | 12,000 |
| Housing (8%) | 7,500 | 0 | 10,200 | 10,101 |
| Retirement (5%) | 5,500 | 921 | 1,616 | 1,915 |
| Life Insurance (4%) | 182 | 85 | 300 | 325 |
| Health Insurance (13%) | 3,879 | 2,731 | 4,097 | 3,054 |
| Vacation/weeks (52%) | 2 | 2 | 3 | 2 |
| Education Funds 23(%) | 273 | 361 | 333 | 454 |
| Auto Allowance (53%) | 71% | 62% | 87% | 53% |

* The percentage following each compensation item indicates the portion of part-time church administrators who received that form of compensation. The averages in each column are for those individuals who actually received that compensation item. Auto allowance is included as part of base salary. See Chapter 3 for a full explanation of how to read this table.

## Total Compensation Comparisons

| Hours Worked Per Week | 1-14 | 15-29 | 30 -39 | All Part-time |
|---|---|---|---|---|
| Average attendance | 306 | 548 | 483 | 456 |
| Average church income | 590,496 | 632,194 | 621,238 | 532,687 |
| Average years employed | 2 | 4 | 5 | 4 |
| Average hours per week | 10 | 20 | 31 | 19 |
| Average compensation | 8,900 | 11,926 | 23,429 | 12,659 |
| Ave. hourly compensation* | 17.11 | 11.47 | 14.53 | 12.81 |
| Average hourly salary** | 13.57 | 12.14 | 11.65 | 11.56 |

Total respondents: 159

* includes base salary, housing or parsonage allowance, retirement contribution, life and health insurance payments, and educational funds (note: auto allowance is included in base salary).

** includes base salary and auto allowance only; see discussion on "rounding errors" in Chapter 3.

# Chapter 8

# *Youth Ministers*

## Employment Profile

On average, youth ministers are employed for a shorter period than other staff members. The typical youth minister is ordained, has a college degree, and is a male. The youth ministers surveyed provided the following statistical profile:

|  | Full-time | Part-time |
|---|---|---|
| Number of Respondents | 560 | 221 |
| Ordained | 71% | 20% |
| Average Years Employed | 4 | 3 |
| Male | 94% | 67% |
| Female | 6% | 33% |
| Self-employed | 3% | 5% |
| Church Employee | 97% | 95% |
| High School Diploma | 5% | 27% |
| Associate Degree | 4% | 7% |
| Bachelor Degree | 58% | 53% |
| Master Degree | 31% | 12% |
| Doctorate | 2% | 1% |

## Compensation Analysis

The analysis below is based upon the tables found later in this chapter. The tables present compensation data according to worship attendance, church income, combinations of size and setting, gender, education, and years employed for youth pastors who serve full-time. The final table provides data for part-time youth pastors based upon the number of hours worked. In this way, the youth pastor's compensation can be viewed from a variety of useful perspectives. The total compensation amount found in a separate box at the bottom of each page was calculated by adding the base salary (including housing allowance), housing or parsonage amount, life and health insurance payments, retirement contribution, and educational funds.

# Key Points

✎ *Church attendance directly impacted the compensation of youth ministers.* Those serving in congregations with an attendance less than 500 are below the national average; those in congregations above 500 are equal to or above the national average. Over one-half of youth ministers serve in the larger churches . *See Table 8-1.*

✎ *Church income impacts total compensation.* Neither church income nor church size, however, is decisive. Compensation leveled off once the church budget exceeded $800,000. The turnover rate for youth ministers is high, regardless of church size or budget. *See Table 8-2.*

✎ *Suburban churches provided the best compensation for smaller congregations.* These congregations provided $4,000 to $6,000 more compensation than did churches in the other geographical categories with an attendance under 500. Yet all youth pastors in churches with an average attendance below 500 were below the national compensation average. *See Table 8-3.*

✎ *Geographical setting did not have a big impact on compensation for larger congregations.* Youth pastors in larger suburban churches earned about $6,000 more than the national average. Compensation levels were fairly comparable across all geographical settings among the larger churches. *See Table 8-4.*

✎ *On average, women received higher salaries than men, although their total compensation was significantly lower.* Overall compensation levels differed by 22%. Male youth ministers outnumbered female youth ministers about 14 to 1. Both groups tended to serve in larger congregations with higher levels of income, but females were paid less than their male counterparts (fringe benefits account for the difference). The disparity in overall earnings appears to be gender related. *See Table 8-5.*

✎ *Educational achievement had a direct impact upon compensation levels of youth ministers, especially for those with graduate degrees.* Ninety-one percent of the youth ministers had a bachelor's degree or higher. Yet, average compensation for those with a bachelor's degree was still below the national average. Having a master's degree or a doctorate resulted in increases in overall compensation. *See Table 8-6.*

✎ *Over 95% of youth pastors served for less than ten years with 80% serving less than five years.* No clear variables exist that differentiate those who serve long periods from those who do not. Those with the longest tenure did receive the highest levels of compensation. *See Table 8-7.*

✎ *In general, part-time youth ministers receive the lowest compensation of part-time professional staff members.* Almost all serve in congregations with an attendance below 400 people. *See Table 8-8.*

# Benefits Analysis

**Full-time staff members.** Full-time youth ministers received benefits similar to other professional staff members. Youth ministers, though, were more likely to receive a housing allowance than those involved in education, music, or church administration.

**Part-time staff members.** Approximately 28% of the youth ministers in this sample worked part-time. Of this group, 32% were female compared to 6% for full-time youth ministers. Part-time workers often serve in smaller churches. Proportionately, salary levels for part-time workers was lower compared to those working full-time. Part-time workers also received only a small fraction of the benefits of full-time staff.

| Benefits | Full-time | Part-time |
|---|---|---|
| ❑ Parsonage provided | 6% | 2% |
| ❑ Housing allowance | 68% | 10% |
| ❑ Retirement | 52% | 7% |
| ❑ Life insurance | 28% | 5% |
| ❑ Health insurance | 76% | 13% |
| ❑ Paid vacation | 94% | 38% |
| ❑ Auto allowance | 76% | 51% |
| ❑ Continuing education funds | 36% | 18% |

# Five Year Compensation Trend: National Averages for Youth Ministers

| | |
|---|---|
| ❑ 1993 | $33,768 |
| ❑ 1994 | $34,238 |
| ❑ 1995 | $35,181 |
| ❑ 1996 | $35,398 |
| ❑ 1997 | $36,968 |

## Table 8-1: Annual Compensation Of Youth Minister By Worship Attendance

| Church Attendance | 0-99 | 100-299 | 300-499 | 500-749 | 750-999 | over 1000 |
|---|---|---|---|---|---|---|
| Number Of Respondents | 0 | 108 | 127 | 118 | 77 | 110 |
| Salary (99%*) | | 18,580 | 21,106 | 23,405 | 24,387 | 24,932 |
| Annual % Increase (66%) | | 7 | 5 | 5 | 5 | 4 |
| Parsonage (6%) | | 8,546 | 8,830 | 6,825 | 7,800 | 10,755 |
| Housing (68%) | | 10,833 | 12,856 | 14,220 | 15,173 | 17,468 |
| Retirement (52%) | | 2,367 | 2,234 | 2,296 | 2,693 | 2,967 |
| Life Insurance (28%) | | 321 | 336 | 418 | 256 | 366 |
| Health Insurance (76%) | | 3,514 | 4,241 | 3,733 | 4,061 | 4,506 |
| Vacation/weeks (94%) | | 2 | 2 | 3 | 3 | 3 |
| Education Funds (36%) | | 925 | 931 | 932 | 991 | 1,321 |
| Auto Allowance (76%) | | 61 | 73 | 80 | 84 | 85 |

* The percentage following each compensation item indicates the portion of church administrators who received that form of compensation. The averages in each column are for those individuals who actually received that compensation item. Auto allowance is included as part of base salary. See Chapter 3 for a full explanation of how to read this table.

## Total Compensation Comparisons

| Church Attendance | 0-99 | 100-299 | 300-499 | 500-749 | 750-999 | Over 1,000 |
|---|---|---|---|---|---|---|
| Average attendance | | 210 | 381 | 593 | 842 | 1,628 |
| Average church income | | 296,628 | 546,250 | 853,434 | 1,284,320 | 2,227,610 |
| Average years employed | | 3 | 3 | 4 | 4 | 5 |
| Average compensation* | | 29,205 | 35,021 | 38,049 | 39,433 | 44,624 |
| Standard deviation | | 11,609 | 12,339 | 11,116 | 9,858 | 12,236 |

National Average for all Youth Ministers: $36,968 with a standard deviation of $12,494 (see Chapter 4, Table 4-3).

Total respondents: 540

* includes base salary, housing or parsonage allowance, retirement contribution, life and health insurance payments, and educational funds (note: auto allowance is included in base salary).

## Table 8-2: Annual Compensation Of Youth Minister By Church Budget

| Church Budget in $ | 0-249,999 | 250,000-499,999 | 500,000-749,000 | 750,000-999,999 | 1,000,000 + |
|---|---|---|---|---|---|
| Number Of Respondents | 52 | 114 | 85 | 68 | 184 |
| Salary (99%*) | 17,160 | 20,368 | 22,319 | 24,585 | 24,974 |
| Annual % Increase (66%) | 7 | 6 | 5 | 5 | 4 |
| Parsonage (6%) | 6,955 | 6,379 | 16,050 | 9,075 | 10,055 |
| Housing (68%) | 9,261 | 12,566 | 12,261 | 15,741 | 16,580 |
| Retirement (52%) | 1,915 | 2,105 | 1,939 | 2,845 | 2,833 |
| Life Insurance (28%) | 396 | 242 | 455 | 466 | 305 |
| Health Insurance (76%) | 3,123 | 4,004 | 3,763 | 4,126 | 4,302 |
| Vacation/weeks (94%) | 2 | 2 | 2 | 3 | 3 |
| Education Funds (36%) | 625 | 940 | 798 | 1,144 | 1,126 |
| Auto Allowance (76%) | 62 | 68 | 71 | 79 | 85 |

* The percentage following each compensation item indicates the portion of church administrators who received that form of compensation. The averages in each column are for those individuals who actually received that compensation item. Auto allowance is included as part of base salary. See Chapter 3 for a full explanation of how to read this table.

## Total Compensation Comparisons

| Church Budget | 0-249,999 | 250,000-499,999 | 500,000-749,999 | 750,000-999,999 | 1,000,000+ |
|---|---|---|---|---|---|
| Average attendance | 252 | 339 | 494 | 672 | 1,229 |
| Average church income | 176,143 | 363,657 | 605,182 | 843,438 | 1,941,563 |
| Average years employed | 3 | 3 | 3 | 4 | 4 |
| Average compensation* | 26,943 | 32,408 | 35,135 | 41,359 | 42,855 |
| Standard deviation | 10,459 | 10,849 | 11,596 | 12,945 | 11,295 |

National Average for all Youth Ministers: $36,968 with a standard deviation of $12,494 (see Chapter 4, Table 4-3).

Total respondents: 503

* includes base salary, housing or parsonage allowance, retirement contribution, life and health insurance payments, and educational funds (note: auto allowance is included in base salary).

## Table 8-3: Annual Compensation Of Youth Minister By Church Setting And Size

| Attendance Under 500 | Urban | Suburban | Medium City | Small Town | Rural |
|---|---|---|---|---|---|
| Number Of Respondents | 23 | 95 | 46 | 57 | 11 |
| Salary (99%*) | 19,485 | 21,566 | 19,238 | 18,159 | 20,993 |
| Annual % Increase (66%) | 4 | 5 | 5 | 6 | 10 |
| Parsonage (6%) | 14,400 | 13,814 | 7,929 | 2,958 | 8,167 |
| Housing (68%) | 12,663 | 13,676 | 11,696 | 9,319 | 10,750 |
| Retirement (52%) | 1,771 | 2,347 | 2,867 | 1,766 | 1,740 |
| Life Insurance (28%) | 129 | 312 | 674 | 164 | 240 |
| Health Insurance (76%) | 3,216 | 4,433 | 3,952 | 3,230 | 3,671 |
| Vacation/weeks (94%) | 2 | 3 | 2 | 2 | 2 |
| Education Funds (36%) | 917 | 1,081 | 931 | 723 | 450 |
| Auto Allowance (76%) | 61 | 69 | 74 | 68 | 45 |

* The percentage following each compensation item indicates the portion of church administrators who received that form of compensation. The averages in each column are for those individuals who actually received that compensation item. Auto allowance is included as part of base salary. See Chapter 3 for a full explanation of how to read this table.

## Total Compensation Comparisons

| Church Size: Under 500 | Urban | Suburban | Medium City | Small Town | Rural |
|---|---|---|---|---|---|
| Average attendance | 304 | 324 | 304 | 284 | 242 |
| Average church income | 520,593 | 495,600 | 423,564 | 327,408 | 235,527 |
| Average years employed | 2 | 4 | 3 | 3 | 3 |
| Average compensation* | 29,956 | 36,537 | 32,732 | 27,263 | 29,953 |
| Standard deviation | 11,074 | 12,786 | 12,010 | 9,499 | 11,966 |

National Average for all Youth Ministers: $36,968 with a standard deviation of $12,494 (see Chapter 4, Table 4-3).

Total respondents: 232

* includes base salary, housing or parsonage allowance, retirement contribution, life and health insurance payments, and educational funds (note: auto allowance is included in base salary).

## Table 8-4: Annual Compensation Of Youth Minister By Church Setting And Size

| Attendance Over 499 | Urban | Suburban | Medium City | Small Town | Rural |
|---|---|---|---|---|---|
| Number Of Respondents | 38 | 139 | 90 | 32 | 2 |
| Salary (99%*) | 23,916 | 24,710 | 23,183 | 25,240 | 28,900 |
| Annual % Increase (66%) | 4 | 5 | 5 | 4 | 4 |
| Parsonage (6%) | 8,825 | 6,555 | 0 | 8,400 | 0 |
| Housing (68%) | 15,899 | 17,349 | 14,551 | 11,460 | 8,000 |
| Retirement (52%) | 3,233 | 2,739 | 2,280 | 2,624 | 4,300 |
| Life Insurance (28%) | 261 | 379 | 435 | 142 | 351 |
| Health Insurance (76%) | 3,459 | 4,356 | 3,871 | 4,191 | 5,512 |
| Vacation/weeks (94%) | 3 | 3 | 3 | 2 | 3 |
| Education Funds (36%) | 1,100 | 1,050 | 1,128 | 1,634 | 750 |
| Auto Allowance (76%) | 84 | 81 | 88 | 78 | 100 |

* The percentage following each compensation item indicates the portion of church administrators who received that form of compensation. The averages in each column are for those individuals who actually received that compensation item. Auto allowance is included as part of base salary. See Chapter 3 for a full explanation of how to read this table.

### Total Compensation Comparisons

| Attendance Over 499 | Urban | Suburban | Medium City | Small Town | Rural |
|---|---|---|---|---|---|
| Average attendance | 986 | 1,148 | 948 | 818 | 1,100 |
| Average church income | 1,517,035 | 1,741,522 | 1,154,603 | 1,138,609 | 1,254,500 |
| Average years employed | 4 | 5 | 3 | 4 | 3 |
| Average compensation* | 37,849 | 43,505 | 38,878 | 38,140 | 41,488 |
| Standard deviation | 11,435 | 12,381 | 9,414 | 11,458 | 2,174 |

National Average for all Youth Ministers: $36,968 with a standard deviation of $12,494 (see Chapter 4, Table 4-3).

Total respondents: 301

* includes base salary, housing or parsonage allowance, retirement contribution, life and health insurance payments, and educational funds (note: auto allowance is included in base salary).

## Table 8-5: Annual Compensation Of Youth Minister By Gender

| Gender | Male | Female |
|---|---|---|
| Number Of Respondents | 521 | 36 |
| Salary (99%*) | 22,286 | 24,466 |
| Annual % Increase (66%) | 5 | 6 |
| Parsonage (6%) | 8,823 | 8,400 |
| Housing (68%) | 14,175 | 11,205 |
| Retirement (52%) | 2,516 | 2,422 |
| Life Insurance (28%) | 360 | 95 |
| Health Insurance (76%) | 4,091 | 2,869 |
| Vacation/weeks (94%) | 3 | 3 |
| Education Funds (36%) | 1,051 | 926 |
| Auto Allowance (76%) | 76 | 75 |

* The percentage following each compensation item indicates the portion of church administrators who received that form of compensation. The averages in each column are for those individuals who actually received that compensation item. Auto allowance is included as part of base salary. See Chapter 3 for a full explanation of how to read this table.

## Total Compensation Comparisons

| Gender | Male | Female |
|---|---|---|
| Average attendance | 712 | 743 |
| Average church income | 1,017,420 | 1,193,522 |
| Average years employed | 4 | 4 |
| Average compensation* | 37,592 | 29,085 |
| Standard deviation | 12,392 | 10,473 |

National Average for all Youth Ministers: $36,968 with a standard deviation of $12,494 (see Chapter 4, Table 4-3).

Total respondents: 557

* includes base salary, housing or parsonage allowance, retirement contribution, life and health insurance payments, and educational funds (note: auto allowance is included in base salary).

## Table 8-6: Annual Compensation Of Youth Minister By Education

| Highest Degree | High School | Associate | Bachelor | Master | Doctorate |
|---|---|---|---|---|---|
| Number Of Respondents | 25 | 17 | 278 | 150 | 8 |
| Salary (99%*) | 20,183 | 21,914 | 21,658 | 24,479 | 29,003 |
| Annual % Increase (66%) | 5 | 6 | 5 | 4 | 4 |
| Parsonage (6%) | 0 | 7,650 | 8,052 | 12,878 | 0 |
| Housing (68%) | 12,630 | 14,298 | 13,958 | 15,047 | 15,906 |
| Retirement (52%) | 960 | 3,164 | 2,289 | 2,829 | 4,036 |
| Life Insurance (28%) | 50 | 302 | 370 | 354 | 555 |
| Health Insurance (76%) | 3,514 | 3,946 | 3,846 | 4,467 | 4,930 |
| Vacation/weeks (94%) | 2 | 2 | 2 | 3 | 3 |
| Education Funds (36%) | 1,083 | 1,043 | 991 | 1,148 | 1,000 |
| Auto Allowance (76%) | 72 | 82 | 78 | 81 | 75 |

* The percentage following each compensation item indicates the portion of church administrators who received that form of compensation. The averages in each column are for those individuals who actually received that compensation item. Auto allowance is included as part of base salary. See Chapter 3 for a full explanation of how to read this table.

## Total Compensation Comparisons

| Highest Degree | High School | Associate | Bachelor | Master | Doctorate |
|---|---|---|---|---|---|
| Average attendance | 438 | 527 | 751 | 746 | 779 |
| Average church income | 679,122 | 823,626 | 1,038,202 | 1,149,392 | 1,511,429 |
| Average years employed | 4 | 4 | 4 | 4 | 5 |
| Average compensation* | 29,444 | 34,913 | 35,618 | 42,169 | 49,597 |
| Standard deviation | 10,688 | 11,332 | 11.609 | 12,155 | 13,106 |

National Average for all Youth Ministers: $36,968 with a standard deviation of $12,494 (see Chapter 4, Table 4-3).

Total respondents: 478

* includes base salary, housing or parsonage allowance, retirement contribution, life and health insurance payments, and educational funds (note: auto allowance is included in base salary).

## Table 8-7: Annual Compensation Of Youth Minister By Years Employed

| Years Employed | 0-5 | 6-10 | 11-15 | over 15 |
|---|---|---|---|---|
| Number Of Respondents | 425 | 80 | 18 | 8 |
| Salary (99%*) | 21,715 | 24,540 | 27,373 | 24,017 |
| Annual % Increase (66%) | 5 | 4 | 5 | 3 |
| Parsonage (6%) | 9,164 | 12,200 | 7,200 | 0 |
| Housing (68%) | 13,341 | 16,127 | 17,437 | 20,860 |
| Retirement (52%) | 2,449 | 2,737 | 2,476 | 3,182 |
| Life Insurance (28%) | 371 | 184 | 114 | 1,167 |
| Health Insurance (76%) | 3,956 | 4,256 | 4,946 | 5,222 |
| Vacation/weeks (94%) | 2 | 3 | 3 | 4 |
| Education Funds (36%) | 1,004 | 1,203 | 1,514 | 467 |
| Auto Allowance (76%) | 74 | 84 | 94 | 100 |

* The percentage following each compensation item indicates the portion of church administrators who received that form of compensation. The averages in each column are for those individuals who actually received that compensation item. Auto allowance is included as part of base salary. See Chapter 3 for a full explanation of how to read this table.

## Total Compensation Comparisons

| Years Employed | 0-5 | 6-10 | 11-15 | Over 15 |
|---|---|---|---|---|
| Average attendance | 678 | 865 | 820 | 1,024 |
| Average church income | 933,594 | 1,423,320 | 1,304,931 | 1,573,337 |
| Average years employed | 2 | 7 | 12 | 19 |
| Average compensation* | 35,522 | 42,214 | 46,275 | 50,238 |
| Standard deviation | 11,914 | 12,337 | 10,835 | 7,848 |

National Average for all Youth Ministers: $36,968 with a standard deviation of $12,494 (see Chapter 4, Table 4-3).

Total respondents: 531

* includes base salary, housing or parsonage allowance, retirement contribution, life and health insurance payments, and educational funds (note: auto allowance is included in base salary).

## Table 8-8: Annual Compensation Of Part-Time Youth Ministers By Hours Worked

| Hours-per-week | 1-14 | 15-29 | 30-39 | All Part-time |
|---|---|---|---|---|
| Number Of Respondents | 25 | 42 | 16 | 221 |
| Salary (90%*) | 5,110 | 9,072 | 13,222 | 9,005 |
| Annual % Increase (36%) | 5 | 4 | 4 | 5 |
| Parsonage (2%) | 7,200 | 3,500 | 0 | 7,820 |
| Housing (10%) | 1,500 | 8,895 | 16,150 | 9,027 |
| Retirement (7%) | 0 | 1,192 | 988 | 1,013 |
| Life Insurance (5%) | 0 | 0 | 207 | 114 |
| Health Insurance (%) | 2,189 | 2,804 | 2,075 | 2,740 |
| Vacation/weeks (38%) | 2 | 2 | 2 | 2 |
| Education Funds (18%) | 438 | 616 | 433 | 502 |
| Auto Allowance (51%) | 60 | 79 | 94 | 51 |

* The percentage following each compensation item indicates the portion of part-time church administrators who received that form of compensation. The averages in each column are for those individuals who actually received that compensation item. Auto allowance is included as part of base salary. See Chapter 3 for a full explanation of how to read this table.

## Total Compensation Comparisons

| Hours Worked Per Week | 1-14 | 15-29 | 30-39 | All Part-time |
|---|---|---|---|---|
| Average attendance | 234 | 267 | 394 | 338 |
| Average church income | 362,105 | 333,680 | 575,422 | 386,237 |
| Average years employed | 2 | 2 | 3 | 3 |
| Average hours per week | 9 | 20 | 30 | 19 |
| Average compensation | 5,850 | 10,257 | 16,243 | 10,264 |
| Ave. hourly compensation* | 12.50 | 9.86 | 10.41 | 10.39 |
| Average hourly salary** | 10.90 | 8.72 | 8.47 | 9.11 |

Total respondents: 221

* includes base salary, housing or parsonage allowance, retirement contribution, life and health insurance payments, and educational funds (note: auto allowance is included in base salary).

** includes base salary and auto allowance only; see discussion of "rounding errors" in Chapter 3.

# Chapter 9

# *Choir and Music Directors*

## Employment Profile

The vast majority of music and choir directors serve on a part-time basis. While men occupy most of the full-time positions, part-time positions divide about equally between males and females. Choir and music directors provided the following employment profile:

|  | Full-time | Part-time |
|---|---|---|
| ☐ Number of Respondents | 356 | 517 |
| ☐ Ordained | 63% | 10% |
| ☐ Average years employed | 7 | 6 |
| ☐ Male | 86% | 53% |
| ☐ Female | 12% | 47% |
| ☐ Self-employed | 2% | 8% |
| ☐ Church Employee | 98% | 92% |
| ☐ High School Diploma | 4% | 13% |
| ☐ Associate's Degree | 4% | 4% |
| ☐ Bachelor's Degree | 46% | 49% |
| ☐ Master's Degree | 40% | 28% |
| ☐ Doctorate | 6% | 6% |

## Compensation Analysis

The analysis below is based upon the tables found later in this chapter. The tables present compensation data according to worship attendance, church income, combinations of size and setting, gender, education, and years employed for music and choir directors who serve full-time. The final table provides data for part-time music and choir directors based upon the number of hours worked. In this way, the compensation of music and choir directors can be viewed from a variety of useful perspectives. The total compensation amount found in a separate box at the bottom of each page was calculated by adding the base salary (including auto allowance), housing or parsonage amount, life and health insurance payments, retirement contribution, and educational funds.

# Key Points

✎ **Compensation increases steadily with church size.** While music and choir directors start out low, they experience the fastest rate of increase of all staff positions. The greatest gains occurred when the attendance reached 100 and 750. *See Table 9-1.*

✎ **Church income impacted compensation in a pattern similar to church attendance.** Again, compensation starts off low, but increases rapidly. A slow down occurs once the income reaches $500,000 but picks back up again at income levels over $750,000 per year. *See Table 9-2.*

✎ **Over the past several years, compensation has fluctuated by geographical setting in smaller congregations.** Last year, urban churches provided the highest compensation for smaller congregations under 500 in attendance. This year, the highest compensations were found in medium size cities. In general, churches with an attendance under 500, provide a compensation package below the national average. *See Table 9-3.*

✎ **More parity existed among the larger churches.** Urban churches provided the highest compensation with churches located in suburbs and medium size cities not far behind. Only churches in small towns were below the national average for those congregations with an attendance above 500. *See Tables 9-4.*

✎ **Male directors earned considerably more than did female directors.** The actual salary difference between men and women was about $4,000, but fewer females received fringe benefits. Also, few women had full-time positions, and those that did tended to work in congregations with lower budgets than their male counterparts. *See Table 9-5.*

✎ **College graduates received substantially higher compensation than did high school graduates; having a graduate degree increased the compensation even more dramatically.** College graduates earned 23% more than those with only a high school education. Significant increases occurred for those having a master's or doctoral degree. *See Table 9-6.*

✎ **Length of employment had minimal impact upon compensation levels.** Those with less than five years of service received a compensation below the national average. This represented 57% of all music and choir directors. Compensation rose steadily with years of service. *See Table 9-7.*

✎ **Most part-time directors work about 13 hours or less per week.** More music and choir directors serve part-time than full-time. Hourly compensation was the highest for those worked 15-29 hours per week. *See Table 9-8.*

# Benefits

**Full-time staff members.** Most fringe benefits were comparable to those of other professional staff members. Fewer also received housing or parsonage allowances, although 57% did receive a housing allowance.

**Part-time staff members.** Part-time workers receive few benefits, but they generally work only about 13 hours per week.

| Benefits Part-time | Full-time | Part-time |
|---|---|---|
| ☐ Housing allowance | 57% | 3% |
| ☐ Parsonage provided | 1% | 0% |
| ☐ Retirement | 54% | 4% |
| ☐ Life insurance | 32% | 2% |
| ☐ Health insurance | 72% | 4% |
| ☐ Paid vacation | 94% | 42% |
| ☐ Auto allowance | 74% | 41% |
| ☐ Continuing education funds | 38% | 15% |

# Five Year Compensation Trend: National Average for Music and Choir Directors

| | | |
|---|---|---|
| ☐ | 1993 | $38,887 |
| ☐ | 1994 | $40,178 |
| ☐ | 1995 | $40,701 |
| ☐ | 1996 | $43,790 |
| ☐ | 1997 | $43,598 |

## Table 9-1: Annual Compensation Of Music or Choir Director By Worship Attendance

| Church Attendance | 0-99 | 100-299 | 300-499 | 500-749 | 750-999 | over 1,000 |
|---|---|---|---|---|---|---|
| Number Of Respondents | 0 | 38 | 60 | 75 | 61 | 107 |
| Salary (99%*) | | 21,524 | 25,524 | 27,324 | 33,128 | 32,844 |
| Annual % Increase (69%) | | 6% | 4% | 4% | 5% | 5% |
| Parsonage (1%) | | 0 | 11,060 | 14,400 | 0 | 20,000 |
| Housing (57%) | | 11,304 | 15,883 | 16,284 | 15,333 | 19,072 |
| Retirement (54%) | | 3,130 | 3,407 | 3,115 | 2,986 | 3,121 |
| Life Insurance (32%) | | 174 | 556 | 530 | 289 | 308 |
| Health Insurance (72%) | | 3,250 | 4,185 | 4,477 | 4,543 | 4,575 |
| Vacation/weeks (94%) | | 2 | 3 | 3 | 3 | 3 |
| Education Funds (38%) | | 1,108 | 871 | 942 | 1,110 | 1,200 |
| Auto Allowance (74%) | | 55% | 60% | 80% | 83% | 8%3 |

* The percentage following each compensation item indicates the portion of all music or choir directors who received that form of compensation. The averages in each column are for those individuals who actually received that compensation item. Auto allowance is included as part of base salary. See Chapter 3 for a full explanation of how to read this table.

## Total Compensation Comparisons

| Worship Attendance | 0-99 | 100-299 | 300-499 | 500-749 | 750-999 | over 1,000 |
|---|---|---|---|---|---|---|
| Average attendance | | 202 | 391 | 597 | 851 | 1,740 |
| Average church income | | 324,046 | 630,237 | 929,050 | 1,297,644 | 2,299,945 |
| Average years employed | | 6 | 7 | 6 | 7 | 7 |
| Average compensation* | | 28,731 | 38,542 | 43,008 | 47,472 | 52,141 |
| Standard deviation | | 12,098 | 13,835 | 17,650 | 12,186 | 15,454 |

National average for all Music Directors: $43,598 with a standard deviation of $15,653 (see Chapter 4, Table 4-3)

Total respondents: 341

* includes base salary, housing or parsonage allowance, retirement contribution, life and health insurance payments,, and educational funds (note: auto allowance is included in base salary)..

## Table 9-2: Annual Compensation Of Music or Choir Director By Church Budget

| Church Budget in $ | 0-249,999 | 250,000-499,999 | 500,000-749,000 | 750,000-999,999 | 1,000,000 + |
|---|---|---|---|---|---|
| Number Of Respondents | 18 | 39 | 51 | 44 | 166 |
| Salary (99%*) | 17,238 | 21,398 | 27,116 | 24,439 | 33,692 |
| Annual % Increase (69%) | 5% | 6% | 4% | 5% | 4% |
| Parsonage (1%) | 0 | 13,920 | 0 | 0 | 20,000 |
| Housing (57%) | 13,192 | 12,605 | 14,216 | 15,600 | 18,584 |
| Retirement (54%) | 2,185 | 3,099 | 2,789 | 2,663 | 3,280 |
| Life Insurance (32%) | 300 | 138 | 1,060 | 903 | 260 |
| Health Insurance (72%) | 2,742 | 3,778 | 3,561 | 4,921 | 4,485 |
| Vacation/weeks (94%) | 2 | 2 | 3 | 3 | 3 |
| Education Funds (38%) | 753 | 957 | 690 | 1,000 | 1,159 |
| Auto Allowance (74%) | 50% | 56% | 61% | 73% | 85% |

\* The percentage following each compensation item indicates the portion of all music or choir directors who received that form of compensation. The averages in each column are for those individuals who actually received that compensation item. Auto allowance is included as part of base salary. See Chapter 3 for a full explanation of how to read this table.

## Total Compensation Comparisons

| Church Budget | 0-249,999 | 250,000-499,999 | 500,000-749,999 | 750,000-999,999 | 1,000,000+ |
|---|---|---|---|---|---|
| Average attendance | 262 | 304 | 522 | 676 | 1,360 |
| Average church income | 153,414 | 354,978 | 619,969 | 843,966 | 2,028,592 |
| Average years employed | 5 | 5 | 7 | 7 | 7 |
| Average compensation* | 22,993 | 31,346 | 38,572 | 39,952 | 51,805 |
| Standard deviation | 13,388 | 11,872 | 12,668 | 13,940 | 14,795 |

National average for all Music Directors: $43,598 with a standard deviation of $15,653 (see Chapter 4, Table 4-3)

Total respondents: 318

\* includes base salary, housing or parsonage allowance, retirement contribution, life and health insurance payments,, and educational funds (note: auto allowance is included in base salary)..

## Table 9-3: Annual Compensation Of Music/Choir Director By Church Setting And Size

| Attendance Under 500 | Urban | Suburban | Medium City | Small Town | Rural |
|---|---|---|---|---|---|
| Number Of Respondents | 17 | 33 | 19 | 26 | 5 |
| Salary (99%*) | 28,742 | 22,070 | 27,064 | 21,258 | 20,832 |
| Annual % Increase (69%) | 4% | 7% | 4% | 5% | 5% |
| Parsonage (1%) | 0 | 11,060 | 0 | 0 | 0 |
| Housing (57%) | 17,284 | 14,800 | 17,116 | 11,968 | 7,800 |
| Retirement (54%) | 2,310 | 2,998 | 3,521 | 4,205 | 3,432 |
| Life Insurance (32%) | 1,355 | 166 | 1,427 | 124 | 97 |
| Health Insurance (72%) | 2,999 | 4,342 | 4,179 | 3,388 | 6,000 |
| Vacation/weeks (94%) | 3 | 3 | 3 | 3 | 2 |
| Education Funds (38%) | 1,078 | 872 | 940 | 960 | 0 |
| Auto Allowance (74%) | 35% | 64% | 68% | 50% | 60% |

* The percentage following each compensation item indicates the portion of all music or choir directors who received that form of compensation. The averages in each column are for those individuals who actually received that compensation item. Auto allowance is included as part of base salary. See Chapter 3 for a full explanation of how to read this table.

## Total Compensation Comparisons

| Attendance Under 500 | Urban | Suburban | Medium City | Small Town | Rural |
|---|---|---|---|---|---|
| Average attendance | 310 | 312 | 347 | 304 | 175 |
| Average church income | 621,563 | 525,773 | 531,162 | 387,494 | 227,112 |
| Average years employed | 9 | 5 | 6 | 9 | 5 |
| Average compensation* | 35,020 | 35,185 | 40,522 | 30,899 | 24,298 |
| Standard deviation | 13,076 | 12,285 | 13,853 | 15,887 | 14,810 |

National average for all Music Directors: $43,598 with a standard deviation of $15,653 (see Chapter 4, Table 4-3)

Total respondents: 100

* includes base salary, housing or parsonage allowance, retirement contribution, life and health insurance payments,, and educational funds (note: auto allowance is included in base salary)..

## Table 9-4: Annual Compensation Of Music/Choir Director By Church Setting And Size

| Attendance Over 499 | Urban | Suburban | Medium City | Small Town | Rural |
|---|---|---|---|---|---|
| Number Of Respondents | 35 | 117 | 64 | 24 | 2 |
| Salary (99%*) | 32,464 | 32,156 | 29,516 | 28,016 | 30,062 |
| Annual % Increase (69%) | 4% | 5% | 5% | 4% | 5% |
| Parsonage (1%) | 0 | 14,400 | 20,000 | 0 | 0 |
| Housing (57%) | 19,532 | 18,256 | 16,624 | 13,428 | 18,000 |
| Retirement (54%) | 3,443 | 3,085 | 2,938 | 2,899 | 4,250 |
| Life Insurance (32%) | 325 | 344 | 519 | 177 | 462 |
| Health Insurance (72%) | 5,687 | 4,339 | 4,390 | 4,415 | 2,197 |
| Vacation/weeks (94%) | 3 | 3 | 3 | 3 | 3 |
| Education Funds (38%) | 1,081 | 1,077 | 1,119 | 1,275 | 900 |
| Auto Allowance (74%) | 83% | 80% | 83% | 83% | 100% |

* The percentage following each compensation item indicates the portion of all music or choir directors who received that form of compensation. The averages in each column are for those individuals who actually received that compensation item. Auto allowance is included as part of base salary. See Chapter 3 for a full explanation of how to read this table.

## Total Compensation Comparisons

| Attendance Over 499 | Urban | Suburban | Medium City | Small Town | Rural |
|---|---|---|---|---|---|
| Average attendance | 958 | 1,309 | 1,058 | 1,058 | 1,100 |
| Average church income | 1,599,873 | 1,922,035 | 1,308,291 | 1,219,472 | 1,254,500 |
| Average years employed | 7 | 7 | 6 | 8 | 4 |
| Average compensation* | 49,945 | 48,836 | 47,617 | 42,357 | 44,516 |
| Standard deviation | 19,571 | 14,257 | 15,064 | 12,536 | 7,183 |

National average for all Music Directors: $43,598 with a standard deviation of $15,653 (see Chapter 4, Table 4-3)

Total respondents: 242

* includes base salary, housing or parsonage allowance, retirement contribution, life and health insurance payments,, and educational funds (note: auto allowance is included in base salary)..

## Table 9-5: Annual Compensation Of Music or Choir Director By Gender

| Gender | Male | Female |
|---|---|---|
| Number Of Respondents | 306 | 49 |
| Salary (99%*) | 29,652 | 25,415 |
| Annual % Increase (69%) | 5% | 5% |
| Parsonage (1%) | 14,040 | 14,400 |
| Housing (57%) | 16,696 | 17,543 |
| Retirement (54%) | 3,169 | 2,745 |
| Life Insurance (32%) | 323 | 1,115 |
| Health Insurance (72%) | 4,470 | 3,110 |
| Vacation/weeks (94%) | 3 | 3 |
| Education Funds (38%) | 1,109 | 768 |
| Auto Allowance (74%) | 75% | 71% |

* The percentage following each compensation item indicates the portion of all music or choir directors who received that form of compensation. The averages in each column are for those individuals who actually received that compensation item. Auto allowance is included as part of base salary. See Chapter 3 for a full explanation of how to read this table.

## Total Compensation Comparisons

| Gender | Male | Female |
|---|---|---|
| Average attendance | 944 | 727 |
| Average church income | 1,380,096 | 999,486 |
| Average years employed | 6 | 7 |
| Average compensation* | 46,020 | 30,646 |
| Standard deviation | 15,838 | 14,208 |

National average for all Music Directors: $43,598 with a standard deviation of $15,653 (see Chapter 4, Table 4-3)

Total respondents  355

* includes base salary, housing or parsonage allowance, retirement contribution, life and health insurance payments,, and educational funds (note: auto allowance is included in base salary)..

## Table 9-6: Annual Compensation Of Music or Choir Director By Education

| Highest Degree | High School | Associate | Bachelor | Master | Doctorate |
|---|---|---|---|---|---|
| Number Of Respondents | 13 | 11 | 133 | 119 | 18 |
| Salary (99%*) | 23,668 | 23,357 | 28,709 | 31,545 | 38,600 |
| Annual % Increase (69%) | 5% | 3% | 5% | 4% | 4% |
| Parsonage (1%) | 0 | 0 | 14,200 | 13,920 | 0 |
| Housing (57%) | 14,233 | 14,950 | 16,797 | 17,446 | 22,995 |
| Retirement (54%) | 3,100 | 3,228 | 2,809 | 3,434 | 4,396 |
| Life Insurance (32%) | 88 | 260 | 517 | 334 | 992 |
| Health Insurance (72%) | 4,772 | 3,732 | 4,283 | 4,586 | 4,934 |
| Vacation/weeks (94%) | 3 | 2 | 3 | 3 | 4 |
| Education Funds (38%) | 700 | 817 | 1,061 | 1,044 | 1,433 |
| Auto Allowance (74%) | 85% | 91% | 71% | 83% | 82% |

* The percentage following each compensation item indicates the portion of all music or choir directors who received that form of compensation. The averages in each column are for those individuals who actually received that compensation item. Auto allowance is included as part of base salary. See Chapter 3 for a full explanation of how to read this table.

## Total Compensation Comparisons

| Highest Degree | High School | Associate | Bachelor | Master | Doctorate |
|---|---|---|---|---|---|
| Average attendance | 1,286 | 619 | 859 | 1,006 | 824 |
| Average church income | 1,282,167 | 1,017,757 | 1,194,483 | 1,556,546 | 2,003,414 |
| Average years employed | 5 | 6 | 6 | 8 | 9 |
| Average compensation* | 37,716 | 34,721 | 42,832 | 49,481 | 51,857 |
| Standard deviation | 13,619 | 16,819 | 13,227 | 17,154 | 20,188 |

National average for all Music Directors: $43,598 with a standard deviation of $15,653 (see Chapter 4, Table 4-3)

Total respondents: 294

* includes base salary, housing or parsonage allowance, retirement contribution, life and health insurance payments,, and educational funds (note: auto allowance is included in base salary)..

### Table 9-7: Annual Compensation Of Music or Choir Director By Years Employed

| Years Employed | 0-5 | 6-10 | 11-15 | over 15 |
|---|---|---|---|---|
| Number Of Respondents | 191 | 83 | 29 | 33 |
| Salary (99%*) | 27,581 | 29,425 | 31,553 | 33,431 |
| Annual % Increase (69%) | 5% | 5% | 4% | 3% |
| Parsonage (1%) | 8,200 | 16,107 | 0 | 0 |
| Housing (57%) | 16,750 | 16,678 | 19,252 | 16,416 |
| Retirement (54%) | 2,956 | 3,017 | 2,839 | 4,322 |
| Life Insurance (32%) | 293 | 548 | 482 | 584 |
| Health Insurance (72%) | 4,174 | 4,339 | 4,468 | 5,104 |
| Vacation/weeks (94%) | 3 | 3 | 4 | 4 |
| Education Funds (38%) | 1,098 | 1,039 | 1,057 | 1,035 |
| Auto Allowance (74%) | 75% | 77% | 76% | 73% |

* The percentage following each compensation item indicates the portion of all music or choir directors who received that form of compensation. The averages in each column are for those individuals who actually received that compensation item. Auto allowance is included as part of base salary. See Chapter 3 for a full explanation of how to read this table.

### Total Compensation Comparisons

| Years Employed | 0-5 | 6-10 | 11-15 | over 15 |
|---|---|---|---|---|
| Average attendance | 893 | 1,009 | 981 | 817 |
| Average church income | 1,230,202 | 1,503,398 | 1,447,193 | 1,567,936 |
| Average years employed | 3 | 8 | 13 | 21 |
| Average compensation* | 42,191 | 45,045 | 45,500 | 50,860 |
| Standard deviation | 14,105 | 16,512 | 20,092 | 18,570 |

National average for all Music Directors: $43,598 with a standard deviation of $15,653 (see Chapter 4, Table 4-3)

Total respondents: 336

* includes base salary, housing or parsonage allowance, retirement contribution, life and health insurance payments,, and educational funds (note: auto allowance is included in base salary)..

## Table 9-8: Annual Compensation Of Part-Time Music/Choir Directors By Hrs. Worked

| Hours-per-week | 1-14 | 15-29 | 30-39 | All Part-time |
|---|---|---|---|---|
| Number Of Respondents | 103 | 64 | 7 | 517 |
| Salary (92%*) | 6,594 | 16,194 | 22,991 | 9,203 |
| Annual % Increase (50%) | 4% | 5% | 4% | 4% |
| Parsonage (0%) | 12,000 | 0 | 0 | 12,000 |
| Housing (3%) | 7,800 | 10,461 | 0 | 10,238 |
| Retirement (4%) | 2,269 | 1,683 | 2,413 | 1,811 |
| Life Insurance (2%) | 0 | 61 | 531 | 270 |
| Health Insurance (4%) | 3,526 | 2,583 | 2,222 | 2,514 |
| Vacation/weeks (42%) | 3 | 2 | 3 | 2 |
| Education Funds (15%) | 394 | 434 | 330 | 410 |
| Auto Allowance (41%) | 56% | 67% | 86% | 41% |

\* The percentage following each compensation item indicates the portion of all part-time music or choir directors who received that form of compensation. The averages in each column are for those individuals who actually received that compensation item. Auto allowance is included as part of base salary. See Chapter 3 for a full explanation of how to read this table.

## Total Compensation Comparisons

| Hours Worked Per Week | 1-14 | 15-29 | 30-39 | All Part-time |
|---|---|---|---|---|
| Average attendance | 261 | 436 | 344 | 299 |
| Average church income | 354,088 | 609,579 | 439,948 | 377,370 |
| Average years employed | 6 | 5 | 8 | 6 |
| Average hours per week | 8 | 19 | 31 | 13 |
| Average compensation | 7,125 | 16,625 | 24,282 | 9,620 |
| Ave. hourly compensation* | 17.13 | 16.83 | 15.06 | 14.23 |
| Average hourly salary** | 15.85 | 16.39 | 14.26 | 13.61 |

Total respondents: 517

\* includes base salary, housing or parsonage allowance, retirement contribution, life and health insurance payments,, and educational funds (note: auto allowance is included in base salary)..

\*\* includes base salary and auto allowance only; see discussion on "rounding errors" in Chapter 3.

# Chapter 10

# *Church Administrators*

## Employment Profile

Church administrators tend to serve in larger churches. Nearly 30% are ordained ministers, although this percentage declines when part-time administrators are included. Men hold most of the full-time positions, but the number of women serving increases for part-time positions. This group of administrators provided the following employment profile:

|  | Full-time | Part-time |
|---|---|---|
| ❐ Number of Respondents | 374 | 118 |
| ❐ Ordained | 29% | 13% |
| ❐ Average years employed | 6 | 5 |
| ❐ Male | 56% | 46% |
| ❐ Female | 44% | 54% |
| ❐ Self-employed | 1% | 6% |
| ❐ Church Employee | 99% | 94% |
| ❐ High School Diploma | 14% | 21% |
| ❐ Associate's Degree | 11% | 14% |
| ❐ Bachelor's Degree | 47% | 40% |
| ❐ Master's Degree | 25% | 20% |
| ❐ Doctorate | 3% | 5% |

## Compensation Analysis

The analysis below is based upon the tables found later in this chapter. The tables present compensation data according to worship attendance, church income, combinations of size and setting, gender, education, and years employed for administrators who serve full-time. The final table provides data for part-time administrators based upon the number of hours worked. In this way, the administrator's compensation can be viewed from a variety of useful perspectives. The total compensation amount found in a separate box at the bottom of each page was calculated by adding the base salary (including auto allowance), housing or parsonage amount, life and health insurance payments, retirement contribution, and educational funds.

# Key Points

✎ *Compensation increased with church size.* Base salary and total compensation increased with church size. Business administrators most often worked in larger churches. About 63% worked in churches with an attendance over 500. About 27% worked in churches over 1,000. The national average compensation corresponded to an attendance of slightly over 700. *See Table 10-1.*

✎ *Church budget had a direct impact on compensation.* Compensation increased rapidly once the church's income exceeded $700,000. Over half of the administrators participating in this study worked in such churches. More than 40% served in congregations with incomes exceeding $1,000,000 per year. *See Table 10-2.*

✎ *Urban, suburban and churches in medium size cities provided the highest compensation for smaller congregations.* Few rural churches employ business administrators. Business administrators in congregations with an attendance under 500 tended to receive compensation levels below the national average regardless of the church's geographical setting. *See Table 10-3.*

✎ *Urban and suburban churches provided the highest compensation for larger churches (attendance above 500).* The majority of administrators in this group work in suburban churches. Those serving in small towns or medium size cities earn less than their urban and suburban counterparts. All, however, were above or near the national average. *See Table 10-4.*

✎ *Male church business administrators received more than 60% higher compensation than did females.* This represented the largest earning gap of any church staff position. In terms of salary alone, women earned almost $8,700 per year less. Women earned far less than the national average even though they served in churches with incomes and attendances that should have reflected higher compensation levels. *See Table 10-5.*

✎ *College graduates received substantially higher compensation than did high school graduates; having a Master's degree increased the compensation even more.* College graduates earned 42% more than those with only a high school education. Significant increases occurred once the administrator earned a master's degree, but compensation declined for those with doctorates. *See Table 10-6.*

✎ *Length of employment had no significant impact upon compensation levels.* Those serving on average 20 years earned about $8,000 more than the national average. Fifty-nine percent of church business administrators had worked for their church an average of three years. *See Table 10-7.*

✎ *Most part-time administrators work about half-time.* On average they earn about 60% of the hourly income of a full-time administrator. This is due to the decreased levels of compensation provided to the increased number of female part-time administrators. *See Table 10-8.*

# Benefits

**Full-time staff members.** Most fringe benefits were slightly less than those of other professional staff members. Fewer church business administrators received housing or parsonage allowances reflecting the mixed ministerial status of this group.

**Part-time staff members.** Twenty-four percent of the church business administrators surveyed worked part-time. Females comprised over half of this group.

| Benefits Part-time | Full-time | Part-time |
|---|---|---|
| ☐ Housing allowance | 23% | 8% |
| ☐ Parsonage provided | 1% | 0% |
| ☐ Retirement | 44% | 13% |
| ☐ Life insurance | 28% | 3% |
| ☐ Health insurance | 60% | 12% |
| ☐ Paid vacation | 94% | 53% |
| ☐ Auto allowance | 73% | 52% |
| ☐ Continuing education funds | 32% | 12% |

# Five Year Compensation Trend: National Averages for Church Administrators

| | |
|---|---|
| ☐ 1993 | $35,333 |
| ☐ 1994 | $37,865 |
| ☐ 1995 | $36,225 |
| ☐ 1996 | $36,871 |
| ☐ 1997 | $37,413 |

## Table 10-1: Annual Compensation Of Administrator By Worship Attendance

| Church Attendance | 0-99 | 100-299 | 300-499 | 500-749 | 750-999 | over 1000 |
|---|---|---|---|---|---|---|
| Number Of Respondents | 3 | 57 | 73 | 72 | 57 | 96 |
| Salary (99%*) | 20,663 | 21,634 | 24,827 | 28,122 | 32,101 | 39,260 |
| Annual % Increase (67%) | 3% | 5% | 5% | 4% | 5% | %4 |
| Parsonage (1%) | 0 | 0 | 8,400 | 0 | 0 | 0 |
| Housing (23%) | 0 | 13,333 | 11,042 | 15,227 | 15,916 | 18,105 |
| Retirement (44%) | 2,459 | 1,805 | 2,645 | 2,597 | 3,246 | 3,406 |
| Life Insurance (28%) | 0 | 411 | 561 | 467 | 215 | 442 |
| Health Insurance (60%) | 2,400 | 2,983 | 3,306 | 3,096 | 3,921 | 4,750 |
| Vacation/weeks (94%) | 3 | 3 | 3 | 3 | 3 | 3 |
| Education Funds (32%) | 0 | 480 | 536 | 801 | 897 | 1,278 |
| Auto Allowance (73%) | 0 | 56% | 66% | 76% | 82% | 84% |

* The percentage following each compensation item indicates the portion of church administrators who received that form of compensation. The averages in each column are for those individuals who actually received that compensation item. Auto allowance is included as part of base salary. See Chapter 3 for a full explanation of how to read this table.

## Total Compensation Comparisons At A Glance*

| Worship Attendance | 0-99 | 100-299 | 300-499 | 500-749 | 750-999 | over 1000 |
|---|---|---|---|---|---|---|
| Average attendance | 58 | 201 | 377 | 610 | 848 | 1,733 |
| Average church income | 138,330 | 327,088 | 575,706 | 927,011 | 1,229,600 | 2,327,694 |
| Average years employed | 9 | 7 | 6 | 6 | 6 | 6 |
| Average compensation* | 22,282 | 23,829 | 29,720 | 35,290 | 41,237 | 51,487 |
| Standard deviation | 11,317 | 9,91 | 12,645 | 11,275 | 12,520 | 16,525 |

National average for all Administrators: $37,413 with a standard deviation of $16,373 (see Chapter 4, Table 4-3)

Total respondents: 358

* includes base salary, housing or parsonage allowance, retirement contribution, life and health insurance payments, and educational funds (note: auto allowance is included in base salary).

*Church Administrators*

## Table 10-2: Annual Compensation Of Administrator By Church Budget

| Church Budget in $ | 0-249,999 | 250,000-499,999 | 500,000-749,000 | 750,000-999,999 | 1,000,000 + |
|---|---|---|---|---|---|
| Number Of Respondents | 34 | 57 | 64 | 37 | 150 |
| Salary (99%*) | 19,001 | 22,913 | 25,879 | 27,625 | 38,092 |
| Annual % Increase (67%) | 4% | 5% | 5% | 4% | 4% |
| Parsonage (1%) | 0 | 0 | 8,400 | 0 | 0 |
| Housing (23%) | 17,500 | 12,012 | 11,995 | 16,527 | 17,139 |
| Retirement (44%) | 2,087 | 1,982 | 2,211 | 2,761 | 3,525 |
| Life Insurance (28%) | 119 | 355 | 541 | 999 | 353 |
| Health Insurance (60%) | 3,094 | 3,097 | 3,033 | 3,724 | 4,373 |
| Vacation/weeks (94%) | 3 | 3 | 3 | 2 | 3 |
| Education Funds (32%) | 511 | 501 | 561 | 701 | 1,161 |
| Auto Allowance (73%) | 41% | 56% | 66% | 84% | 86% |

* The percentage following each compensation item indicates the portion of church administrators who received that form of compensation. The averages in each column are for those individuals who actually received that compensation item. Auto allowance is included as part of base salary. See Chapter 3 for a full explanation of how to read this table.

## Total Compensation Comparisons

| Church Budget | 0-249,999 | 250,000-499,999 | 500,000-749,999 | 750,000-999,999 | 1,000,000+ |
|---|---|---|---|---|---|
| Average attendance | 262 | 386 | 508 | 716 | 1,331 |
| Average church income | 150,295 | 373,454 | 617,388 | 857,994 | 2,070,291 |
| Average years employed | 8 | 6 | 6 | 5 | 6 |
| Average compensation* | 22,031 | 26,493 | 31,822 | 36,491 | 48,982 |
| Standard deviation | 11,020 | 9,610 | 10,375 | 12,618 | 16,792 |

National average for all Administrators: $37,413 with a standard deviation of $16,373 (see Chapter 4, Table 4-3)

Total respondents: 342

* includes base salary, housing or parsonage allowance, retirement contribution, life and health insurance payments, and educational funds (note: auto allowance is included in base salary).

### Table 10-3: Annual Compensation Of Administrator By Church Setting And Size

| Attendance Under 500 | Urban | Suburban | Medium City | Small Town | Rural |
|---|---|---|---|---|---|
| Number Of Respondents | 19 | 41 | 37 | 31 | 5 |
| Salary (99%*) | 24,766 | 24,512 | 24,833 | 20,695 | 14,781 |
| Annual % Increase (67%) | 4% | 5% | 6% | 4% | 4% |
| Parsonage (1%) | 0 | 8,400 | 0 | 0 | 0 |
| Housing (23%) | 5,150 | 14,557 | 7,800 | 12,533 | 13,000 |
| Retirement (44%) | 2,792 | 2,396 | 2,488 | 2,184 | 1,086 |
| Life Insurance (28%) | 138 | 383 | 859 | 480 | 2,038 |
| Health Insurance (60%) | 1,992 | 3,768 | 3,470 | 2,584 | 3,000 |
| Vacation/weeks (94%) | 2 | 3 | 3 | 3 | 3 |
| Education Funds (32%) | 690 | 358 | 519 | 534 | 0 |
| Auto Allowance (73%) | 53% | 61% | 57% | 71% | 40% |

* The percentage following each compensation item indicates the portion of church administrators who received that form of compensation. The averages in each column are for those individuals who actually received that compensation item. Auto allowance is included as part of base salary. See Chapter 3 for a full explanation of how to read this table.

### Total Compensation Comparisons

| Attendance Under 500 | Urban | Suburban | Medium City | Small Town | Rural |
|---|---|---|---|---|---|
| Average attendance | 331 | 290 | 308 | 263 | 281 |
| Average church income | 608,321 | 557,200 | 380,304 | 315,168 | 297,628 |
| Average years employed | 5 | 7 | 7 | 8 | 6 |
| Average compensation* | 27,201 | 30,046 | 27,116 | 24,159 | 18,823 |
| Standard deviation | 12,773 | 10,940 | 10,774 | 12,575 | 4,268 |

National average for all Administrators: $37,413 with a standard deviation of $16,373 (see Chapter 4, Table 4-3)

Total respondents: 133

* includes base salary, housing or parsonage allowance, retirement contribution, life and health insurance payments, and educational funds (note: auto allowance is included in base salary).

## Table 10-4: Annual Compensation Of Administrator By Church Setting And Size

| Attendance Over 499 | Urban | Suburban | Medium City | Small Town | Rural |
|---|---|---|---|---|---|
| Number Of Respondents | 33 | 100 | 68 | 20 | 2 |
| Salary (99%*) | 35,896 | 39,211 | 27,254 | 30,392 | 26,150 |
| Annual % Increase (67%) | 5% | 4% | 4% | 4% | 5% |
| Parsonage (1%) | 0 | 0 | 0 | 0 | 0 |
| Housing (23%) | 19,944 | 17,230 | 15,559 | 15,847 | 14,400 |
| Retirement (44%) | 3,319 | 3,161 | 2,842 | 3,943 | 0 |
| Life Insurance (28%) | 319 | 402 | 547 | 213 | 200 |
| Health Insurance (60%) | 4,192 | 4,325 | 3,595 | 3,786 | 5,316 |
| Vacation/weeks (94%) | 3 | 3 | 3 | 3 | 3 |
| Education Funds (32%) | 1,125 | 1,090 | 1,000 | 830 | 1,000 |
| Auto Allowance (73%) | 88% | 79% | 84% | 75% | 100% |

* The percentage following each compensation item indicates the portion of church administrators who received that form of compensation. The averages in each column are for those individuals who actually received that compensation item. Auto allowance is included as part of base salary. See Chapter 3 for a full explanation of how to read this table.

### Total Compensation Comparisons

| Attendance Over 499 | Urban | Suburban | Medium City | Small Town | Rural |
|---|---|---|---|---|---|
| Average attendance | 992 | 1,350 | 1,020 | 913 | 900 |
| Average church income | 1,648,074 | 1,992,318 | 1,172,531 | 1,242,222 | 954,500 |
| Average years employed | 6 | 6 | 5 | 7 | 4 |
| Average compensation* | 46,804 | 49,173 | 36,458 | 41,808 | 39,266 |
| Standard deviation | 23,201 | 15,673 | 12,218 | 13,226 | 1,039 |

National average for all Administrators: $37,413 with a standard deviation of $16,373 (see Chapter 4, Table 4-3)

Total respondents: 223

* includes base salary, housing or parsonage allowance, retirement contribution, life and health insurance payments, and educational funds (note: auto allowance is included in base salary).

### Table 10-5: Annual Compensation Of Administrator By Gender

| Gender | Male | Female |
|---|---|---|
| Number Of Respondents | 209 | 164 |
| Salary (99%*) | 33,961 | 25,276 |
| Annual % Increase (67%) | 5% | 4% |
| Parsonage (1%) | 8,400 | 0 |
| Housing (23%) | 16,266 | 10,015 |
| Retirement (44%) | 3,214 | 2,505 |
| Life Insurance (28%) | 430 | 470 |
| Health Insurance (60%) | 4,355 | 2,721 |
| Vacation/weeks (94%) | 3 | 3 |
| Education Funds (32%) | 1,063 | 596 |
| Auto Allowance (73%) | 81% | 63% |

* The percentage following each compensation item indicates the portion of church administrators who received that form of compensation. The averages in each column are for those individuals who actually received that compensation item. Auto allowance is included as part of base salary. See Chapter 3 for a full explanation of how to read this table.

### Total Compensation Comparisons

| Gender | Male | Female |
|---|---|---|
| Average attendance | 1,039 | 555 |
| Average church income | 1,537,785 | 716,302 |
| Average years employed | 6 | 7 |
| Average compensation* | 45,394 | 27,845 |
| Standard deviation | 16,758 | 11,298 |

National average for all Administrators: $37,413 with a standard deviation of $16,373 (see Chapter 4, Table 4-3)

Total respondents 373

* includes base salary, housing or parsonage allowance, retirement contribution, life and health insurance payments, and educational funds (note: auto allowance is included in base salary).

## Table 10-6: Annual Compensation Of Administrator By Education

| Highest Degree | High School | Associate | Bachelor | Master | Doctorate |
|---|---|---|---|---|---|
| Number Of Respondents | 44 | 33 | 146 | 76 | 8 |
| Salary (99%*) | 22,654 | 24,492 | 31,552 | 35,436 | 34,998 |
| Annual % Increase (67%) | 5% | 4% | 4% | 5% | 5% |
| Parsonage (1%) | 0 | 0 | 8,400 | 8,400 | 0 |
| Housing (23%) | 11,240 | 14,739 | 17,597 | 16,702 | 20,000 |
| Retirement (44%) | 2,530 | 1,712 | 2,968 | 3,638 | 3,275 |
| Life Insurance (28%) | 1,153 | 208 | 442 | 390 | 165 |
| Health Insurance (60%) | 3,304 | 3,130 | 4,004 | 4,437 | 3,047 |
| Vacation/weeks (94%) | 3 | 3 | 3 | 3 | 4 |
| Education Funds (32%) | 523 | 571 | 902 | 1,033 | 1,900 |
| Auto Allowance (73%) | 64% | 73% | 74% | 80% | 75% |

* The percentage following each compensation item indicates the portion of church administrators who received that form of compensation. The averages in each column are for those individuals who actually received that compensation item. Auto allowance is included as part of base salary. See Chapter 3 for a full explanation of how to read this table.

## Total Compensation Comparisons

| Highest Degree | High School | Associate | Bachelor | Master | Doctorate |
|---|---|---|---|---|---|
| Average attendance | 474 | 656 | 877 | 1,138 | 772 |
| Average church income | 914,330 | 869,728 | 1,199,079 | 1,643,233 | 927,460 |
| Average years employed | 7 | 7 | 6 | 5 | 7 |
| Average compensation* | 27,301 | 30,668 | 38,825 | 47,487 | 42,864 |
| Standard deviation | 14,866 | 13,132 | 16,620 | 17,942 | 12,349 |

National average for all Administrators: $37,413 with a standard deviation of $16,373 (see Chapter 4, Table 4-3)

Total respondents: 307

* includes base salary, housing or parsonage allowance, retirement contribution, life and health insurance payments, and educational funds (note: auto allowance is included in base salary).

## Table 10-7: Annual Compensation Of Administrator By Years Employed

| Years Employed | 0-5 | 6-10 | 11-15 | over 15 |
|---|---|---|---|---|
| Number Of Respondents | 217 | 84 | 36 | 27 |
| Salary (99%*) | 29,225 | 28,556 | 31,879 | 36,262 |
| Annual % Increase (67%) | 5% | 4% | 4% | 4% |
| Parsonage (1%) | 8,400 | 0 | 0 | 0 |
| Housing (23%) | 15,028 | 17,811 | 15,901 | 14,000 |
| Retirement (44%) | 2,492 | 2,975 | 3,474 | 3,843 |
| Life Insurance (28%) | 441 | 477 | 263 | 635 |
| Health Insurance (60%) | 3,678 | 3,727 | 4,528 | 4,204 |
| Vacation/weeks (94%) | 3 | 3 | 4 | 4 |
| Education Funds (32%) | 856 | 960 | 754 | 855 |
| Auto Allowance (73%) | 75% | 73% | 67% | 74% |

* The percentage following each compensation item indicates the portion of church administrators who received that form of compensation. The averages in each column are for those individuals who actually received that compensation item. Auto allowance is included as part of base salary. See Chapter 3 for a full explanation of how to read this table.

## Total Compensation Comparisons

| Years Employed | 0-5 | 6-10 | 11-15 | over 15 |
|---|---|---|---|---|
| Average attendance | 841 | 835 | 783 | 805 |
| Average church income | 1,123,573 | 1,170,419 | 1,471,218 | 1,504,726 |
| Average years employed | 3 | 8 | 13 | 19 |
| Average compensation* | 35,841 | 37,181 | 40,024 | 45,612 |
| Standard deviation | 15,122 | 18,769 | 15,980 | 20,686 |

National average for all Administrators: $37,413 with a standard deviation of $16,373 (see Chapter 4, Table 4-3)

Total respondents: 364

* includes base salary, housing or parsonage allowance, retirement contribution, life and health insurance payments, and educational funds (note: auto allowance is included in base salary).

## Table 10-8: Annual Compensation Of Part-Time Administrators By Hours Worked

| Hours-per-week | 1-14 | 15-29 | 30-39 | All Part-time |
|---|---|---|---|---|
| Number Of Respondents | 4 | 27 | 21 | 118 |
| Salary (92%*) | 3,220 | 12,998 | 17,435 | 12,861 |
| Annual % Increase (59%) | 5% | 7% | 4% | 6% |
| Parsonage (0%) | 0 | 0 | 0 | 0 |
| Housing (8%) | 0 | 7,522 | 16,863 | 11,131 |
| Retirement (13%) | 0 | 1,366 | 3,485 | 1,924 |
| Life Insurance (3%) | 0 | 270 | 546 | 477 |
| Health Insurance (12%) | 0 | 1,164 | 3,601 | 2,514 |
| Vacation/weeks (53%) | 1 | 2 | 2 | 2 |
| Education Funds (12%) | 0 | 338 | 379 | 421 |
| Auto Allowance (52%) | 75% | 59% | 76% | 52% |

* The percentage following each compensation item indicates the portion of part-time church administrators who received that form of compensation. The averages in each column are for those individuals who actually received that compensation item. Auto allowance is included as part of base salary. See Chapter 3 for a full explanation of how to read this table.

## Total Compensation Comparisons

| Hours Worked Per Week | 1-14 | 15-29 | 30-39 | All Part-time |
|---|---|---|---|---|
| Average attendance | 272 | 423 | 565 | 451 |
| Average church income | 285,500 | 571,041 | 726,161 | 570,732 |
| Average years employed | 2 | 4 | 5 | 5 |
| Average hours per week | 7 | 21 | 31 | 24 |
| Average compensation | 3,220 | 13,165 | 20,541 | 14,027 |
| Ave. hourly compensation** | 8.85 | 12.06 | 12.74 | 11.24 |
| Average hourly salary* | 8.85 | 11.90 | 10.82 | 10.31 |

Total respondents: 118

* includes base salary, housing or parsonage allowance, retirement contribution, life and health insurance payments, and educational funds (note: auto allowance is included in base salary).

* includes base salary and auto allowance only; see discussion on "rounding errors" in Chapter 3.

# Chapter 11

# *Church Bookkeepers*

## Employment Profile

From an employment standpoint, church bookkeepers are aligned with church secretaries and custodians. Very few are ordained ministers. They tend to be hourly paid church employees with the overwhelming number female, whether full-time or part-time. An increasing number are college graduates. The church bookkeepers surveyed provided the following employment profile:

|  | Full-time | Part-time |
|---|---|---|
| Number of Respondents | 305 | 329 |
| Ordained | 3% | 1% |
| Average years employed | 8 | 6 |
| Male | 10% | 17% |
| Female | 90% | 83% |
| Self-employed | 0% | 6% |
| Church Employee | 100% | 94% |
| High School Diploma | 45% | 32% |
| Associate Degree | 16% | 12% |
| Bachelor Degree | 36% | 45% |
| Master Degree | 2% | 10% |
| Doctorate | 1% | 1% |

## Compensation Analysis

The analysis below is based upon the tables found later in this chapter. The tables present compensation data according to worship attendance, church income, combinations of size and setting, gender, education, and years employed for bookkeepers who serve full-time. The final table provides data for part-time bookkeepers based upon the number of hours worked. In this way, the bookkeeper's compensation can be viewed from a variety of useful perspectives. The total compensation amount found in a separate box at the bottom of each page was calculated by adding the base salary (including auto allowance), housing or parsonage amount, life and health insurance payments, retirement contribution, and educational funds.

## Key Points

✎ *The compensation of bookkeepers increased significantly only in the largest churches.* Total compensation increases very slowly with attendance, with the fastest growth occurring once church attendance exceeds 1,000. Over 30% of all church bookkeepers worked in churches of that size or larger. *See Table 11-1.*

✎ *Once church income hit $200,000, compensation growth slowed or declined until the church's income exceeded $750,000.* At that point bookkeeper compensation increased. The national average compensation was not achieved until the church's income was over $800,000. *See Table 11-2.*

✎ *Suburban churches provided the highest compensation for bookkeepers in smaller churches (attendance under 500).* Those churches with an average attendance under 500 provided compensations below the national average. *See Tables 11-3.*

✎ *Urban churches provided the highest compensation for bookkeepers in larger churches (attendance over 500).* In churches with an average attendance over 500, only those in suburban or urban settings exceeded the national average. *See Tables 11-4.*

✎ *Male bookkeepers earned considerably more than did females.* This was true even though men represented only 10% of all bookkeepers. On average, they earned 15% more than did their female counterparts. Both men and women tended to work in larger congregations. *See Table 11-5.*

✎ *Educational achievement had little impact on total compensation.* Bookkeepers with college degrees earned about 7% more than the national average. Having a master's degree did not increase income over the bachelor's degree. Yet, those with less education had served for longer periods of time. *See Table 11-6.*

✎ *Length of employment had little impact upon the compensation of church bookkeepers.* About 45% of all full-time bookkeepers had worked an average of three years at their church. These individuals earned earned $2,300 less than the group with an average of 22 years of service. *See Table 11-7.*

✎ *Most part-time bookkeepers work about between 19-29 hours per week.* Their average hourly compensation is comparable to that of secretaries and custodians, but less than the other staff positions examined in this study. *See Table 11-8.*

# Benefit Analysis

**Full-time staff members.** Church bookkeepers received less benefits than did administrators or ministerial staff. The percentage of those who received health insurance, retirement contributions, or educational funds was notably less. Very few received any housing allowance. Bookkeepers, however, did receive better benefits than either secretaries or custodians.

**Part-time staff members.** Over half of the bookkeepers surveyed worked part-time for their churches. The majority worked between 15-29 hours per week. Over 80% of part-time bookkeepers were women. Part-time bookkeepers earned less than other part-time professional staff, and about the same as secretaries and custodians. As with other part-time positions, few received fringe benefits other than vacation.

| Benefits | Full-time | Part-time |
|---|---|---|
| ☐ Housing allowance | 2% | 1% |
| ☐ Parsonage provided | 0% | 0% |
| ☐ Retirement | 32% | 6% |
| ☐ Life insurance | 29% | 3% |
| ☐ Health insurance | 50% | 6% |
| ☐ Paid vacation | 92% | 37% |
| ☐ Auto allowance | 66% | 45% |
| ☐ Continuing education funds | 14% | 7% |

# Five Year Compensation Trend: National Averages for Bookkeepers

| | | |
|---|---|---|
| ☐ | 1993 | $20,300 |
| ☐ | 1994 | $23,172 |
| ☐ | 1995 | $22,106 |
| ☐ | 1996 | $23,548 |
| ☐ | 1997 | $23,839 |

## Table 11-1: Annual Compensation Of Bookkeeper By Worship Attendance

| Church Attendance | 0-99 | 100-299 | 300-499 | 500-749 | 750-999 | over 1,000 |
|---|---|---|---|---|---|---|
| Number Of Respondents | 0 | 30 | 40 | 58 | 44 | 83 |
| Salary (97%*) | | 18,971 | 18,855 | 20,898 | 21,101 | 24,206 |
| Annual % Increase (69%) | | 6% | 4% | 4% | 5% | 4% |
| Parsonage (0%) | | 0 | 0 | 0 | 0 | 0 |
| Housing (2%) | | 0 | 9,600 | 17,160 | 0 | 26,200 |
| Retirement (32%) | | 1,659 | 1,872 | 1,504 | 1,494 | 1,627 |
| Life Insurance (29%) | | 790 | 325 | 450 | 168 | 198 |
| Health Insurance (50%) | | 2.391 | 2,306 | 2,788 | 2,988 | 3,391 |
| Vacation/weeks (92%) | | 2 | 3 | 3 | 3 | 3 |
| Education Funds (14%) | | 500 | 290 | 571 | 300 | 563 |
| Auto Allowance (66%) | | 40% | 53% | 66% | 66% | 83% |

* The percentage following each compensation item indicates the portion of all church bookkeepers who received that form of compensation. The averages in each column are for those individuals who actually received that compensation item. Auto allowance is included as part of base salary. See Chapter 3 for a full explanation of how to read this table.

## Total Compensation Comparisons

| Worship Attendance | 0-99 | 100-299 | 300-499 | 500-749 | 750-999 | over 1,000 |
|---|---|---|---|---|---|---|
| Average attendance | | 194 | 392 | 590 | 842 | 1,755 |
| Average church income | | 361,969 | 650,554 | 1,010,980 | 1,392,558 | 2,431,103 |
| Average years employed | | 7 | 9 | 8 | 7 | 8 |
| Average compensation* | | 20,002 | 20,494 | 23,119 | 22,857 | 27,531 |
| Standard deviation | | 6,864 | 7,005 | 6,314 | 7,596 | 7,494 |

National average for all bookkeepers: $23,839 with a standard deviation of $7,890 (see Chapter 4, Table 4-3)

Total respondents: 255

* includes base salary, housing or parsonage allowance, retirement contribution, life and health insurance payments, and educational funds (note: auto allowance is included in base salary).

## Table 11-2: Annual Compensation Of Bookkeeper By Church Budget

| Church Budget in $ | 0-249,999 | 250,000-499,999 | 500,000-749,000 | 750,000-999,999 | 1,000,000 + |
|---|---|---|---|---|---|
| Number Of Respondents | 8 | 26 | 38 | 26 | 132 |
| Salary(97%*) | 17,410 | 18,789 | 18,794 | 20,919 | 23,625 |
| Annual % Increase (69%) | 7% | 5% | 5% | 3% | 5% |
| Parsonage (0%) | 0 | 0 | 0 | 0 | 0 |
| Housing (2%) | 0 | 9,600 | 0 | 17,160 | 26,200 |
| Retirement (32%) | 1,500 | 1,840 | 1,455 | 1,618 | 1,670 |
| Life Insurance (29%) | 0 | 450 | 219 | 752 | 210 |
| Health Insurance (50%) | 2,400 | 1,965 | 1,961 | 3,392 | 3,300 |
| Vacation/weeks (92%) | 2 | 3 | 2 | 3 | 3 |
| Education Funds (14%) | 500 | 462 | 370 | 250 | 525 |
| Auto Allowance (66%) | 25% | 42% | 50% | 62% | 78% |

* The percentage following each compensation item indicates the portion of all church bookkeepers who received that form of compensation. The averages in each column are for those individuals who actually received that compensation item. Auto allowance is included as part of base salary. See Chapter 3 for a full explanation of how to read this table.

## Total Compensation Comparisons

| Church Budget | 0-249,999 | 250,000-499,999 | 500,000-749,999 | 750,000-999,999 | 1,000,000+ |
|---|---|---|---|---|---|
| Average attendance | 196 | 352 | 524 | 665 | 1,339 |
| Average church income | 165,375 | 372,662 | 609,567 | 837,608 | 2,123,951 |
| Average years employed | 4 | 9 | 8 | 8 | 8 |
| Average compensation* | 18,041 | 20,479 | 19,913 | 23,665 | 26,648 |
| Standard deviation | 7,534 | 5,738 | 6,877 | 5,373 | 8,117 |

National average for all bookkeepers: $23,839 with a standard deviation of $7,890 (see Chapter 4, Table 4-3)

Total respondents: 230

* includes base salary, housing or parsonage allowance, retirement contribution, life and health insurance payments, and educational funds (note: auto allowance is included in base salary).

## Table 11-3: Annual Compensation Of Bookkeeper By Church Setting And Size

| Attendance Under 500 | Urban | Suburban | Medium City | Small Town | Rural |
|---|---|---|---|---|---|
| Number Of Respondents | 12 | 15 | 19 | 21 | 2 |
| Salary(97%*) | 17,991 | 20,106 | 19,296 | 18,488 | 15,600 |
| Annual % Increase (69%) | 4% | 5% | 5% | 4% | 10% |
| Parsonage (0%) | 0 | 0 | 0 | 0 | 0 |
| Housing (2%) | 0 | 0 | 9,600 | 0 | 0 |
| Retirement (32%) | 1,631 | 1,630 | 2,145 | 1,686 | 0 |
| Life Insurance (29%) | 0 | 194 | 414 | 1,082 | 0 |
| Health Deductible (50%) | 2,558 | 2,831 | 2,402 | 1,778 | 0 |
| Vacation/weeks (92%) | 3 | 2 | 3 | 2 | 2 |
| Education Funds (14%) | 300 | 300 | 450 | 317 | 0 |
| Auto Allowance (66%) | 33% | 73% | 53% | 29% | 50% |

* The percentage following each compensation item indicates the portion of all church bookkeepers who received that form of compensation. The averages in each column are for those individuals who actually received that compensation item. Auto allowance is included as part of base salary. See Chapter 3 for a full explanation of how to read this table.

## Total Compensation Comparisons

| Attendance Under 500 | Urban | Suburban | Medium City | Small Town | Rural |
|---|---|---|---|---|---|
| Average attendance | 313 | 313 | 349 | 280 | 150 |
| Average church income | 673,400 | 573,752 | 441,394 | 494,478 | 125,000 |
| Average years employed | 8 | 9 | 10 | 7 | 2 |
| Average compensation* | 19,414 | 21,946 | 21,933 | 18,556 | 15,600 |
| Standard deviation | 7,274 | 5,472 | 7,499 | 6,065 | 11,030 |

National average for all bookkeepers: $23,839 with a standard deviation of $7,890 (see Chapter 4, Table 4-3)

Total respondents: 69

* includes base salary, housing or parsonage allowance, retirement contribution, life and health insurance payments, and educational funds (note: auto allowance is included in base salary).

## Table 11-4: Annual Compensation Of Bookkeeper By Church Setting And Size

| Attendance Over 499 | Urban | Suburban | Medium City | Small Town | Rural |
|---|---|---|---|---|---|
| Number Of Respondents | 24 | 86 | 46 | 25 | 3 |
| Salary(97%*) | 24,247 | 23,880 | 20,611 | 19,397 | 20,337 |
| Annual % Increase (69%) | 5% | 4% | 5% | 4% | 6% |
| Parsonage (0%) | 0 | 0 | 0 | 0 | 0 |
| Housing (2%) | 0 | 26,200 | 17,160 | 0 | 0 |
| Retirement (32%) | 1,748 | 1,648 | 1,392 | 1,210 | 3,000 |
| Life Insurance (29%) | 152 | 186 | 480 | 161 | 200 |
| Health Insurance (50%) | 3,277 | 3,142 | 3,270 | 2,580 | 3,366 |
| Vacation/weeks (92%) | 3 | 3 | 3 | 2 | 2 |
| Education Funds (14%) | 700 | 529 | 340 | 450 | 300 |
| Auto Allowance (66%) | 67% | 77% | 67% | 76% | 100% |

* The percentage following each compensation item indicates the portion of all church bookkeepers who received that form of compensation. The averages in each column are for those individuals who actually received that compensation item. Auto allowance is included as part of base salary. See Chapter 3 for a full explanation of how to read this table.

## Total Compensation Comparisons

| Attendance Over 499 | Urban | Suburban | Medium City | Small Town | Rural |
|---|---|---|---|---|---|
| Average attendance | 894 | 1,343 | 1,090 | 1,044 | 967 |
| Average church income | 1,742,725 | 2,138,581 | 1,441,763 | 1,091,846 | 1,019,667 |
| Average years employed | 6 | 7 | 9 | 6 | 6 |
| Average compensation* | 27,236 | 26,770 | 23,022 | 21,073 | 23,747 |
| Standard deviation | 9,460 | 8,078 | 4,623 | 5,987 | 616 |

National average for all bookkeepers: $23,839 with a standard deviation of $7,890 (see Chapter 4, Table 4-3)

Total respondents: 184

* includes base salary, housing or parsonage allowance, retirement contribution, life and health insurance payments, and educational funds (note: auto allowance is included in base salary).

## Table 11-5: Annual Compensation Of Bookkeeper By Gender

| Gender | Male | Female |
|---|---|---|
| Number Of Respondents | 26 | 235 |
| Salary(97%*) | 22,704 | 21,477 |
| Annual % Increase (69%) | 6% | 5% |
| Parsonage (0%) | 0 | 0 |
| Housing (2%) | 26,200 | 13,380 |
| Retirement (32%) | 1,511 | 1,644 |
| Life Insurance (29%) | 187 | 319 |
| Health Insurance (50%) | 4,277 | 2,855 |
| Vacation/weeks (92%) | 2 | 3 |
| Education Funds (14%) | 1,167 | 406 |
| Auto Allowance (66%) | 69% | 66% |

* The percentage following each compensation item indicates the portion of all church bookkeepers who received that form of compensation. The averages in each column are for those individuals who actually received that compensation item. Auto allowance is included as part of base salary. See Chapter 3 for a full explanation of how to read this table.

## Total Compensation Comparisons

| Gender | Male | Female |
|---|---|---|
| Average attendance | 1,055 | 924 |
| Average church income | 1,413,222 | 1,474,133 |
| Average years employed | 5 | 8 |
| Average compensation* | 27,176 | 23,517 |
| Standard deviation | 12,900 | 7,106 |

National average for all bookkeepers: $23,839 with a standard deviation of $7,890 (see Chapter 4, Table 4-3)

Total respondents: 261

* includes base salary, housing or parsonage allowance, retirement contribution, life and health insurance payments, and educational funds (note: auto allowance is included in base salary).

## Table 11-6: Annual Compensation Of Bookkeeper By Education

| Highest Degree | High School | Associate | Bachelor | Master | Doctorate |
|---|---|---|---|---|---|
| Number Of Respondents | 82 | 30 | 65 | 4 | 0 |
| Salary(97%*) | 22,066 | 19,918 | 22,878 | 21,252 | |
| Annual % Increase (69%) | 4% | 5% | 5% | 6% | |
| Parsonage (0%) | 0 | 0 | 0 | 0 | |
| Housing (2%) | 9,600 | 0 | 18,000 | 0 | |
| Retirement (32%) | 1,650 | 1,283 | 1,739 | 591 | |
| Life Insurance (29%) | 517 | 82 | 219 | 104 | |
| Health Insurance (50%) | 3,035 | 2,751 | 3,091 | 645 | |
| Vacation/weeks (92%) | 3 | 2 | 3 | 2 | |
| Education Funds (14%) | 373 | 450 | 662 | 0 | |
| Auto Allowance (66%) | 68% | 67% | 69% | 50% | |

* The percentage following each compensation item indicates the portion of all church bookkeepers who received that form of compensation. The averages in each column are for those individuals who actually received that compensation item. Auto allowance is included as part of base salary. See Chapter 3 for a full explanation of how to read this table.

## Total Compensation Comparisons

| Highest Degree | High School | Associate | Bachelor | Master | Doctorate |
|---|---|---|---|---|---|
| Average attendance | 972 | 921 | 1,135 | 618 | |
| Average church income | 1,479,682 | 1,432,834 | 1,789,338 | 587,959 | |
| Average years employed | 10 | 6 | 5 | 5 | |
| Average compensation* | 24,453 | 21,723 | 25,608 | 21,760 | |
| Standard deviation | 7,233 | 4,600 | 8,628 | 4,181 | |

National average for all bookkeepers: $23,839 with a standard deviation of $7,890 (see Chapter 4, Table 4-3)

Total respondents: 181

* includes base salary, housing or parsonage allowance, retirement contribution, life and health insurance payments, and educational funds (note: auto allowance is included in base salary).

### Table 11-7: Annual Compensation Of Bookkeeper By Years Employed

| Years Employed | 0-5 | 6-10 | 11-15 | over 15 |
|---|---|---|---|---|
| Number Of Respondents | 116 | 78 | 32 | 32 |
| Salary(97%*) | 20,891 | 21,571 | 22,947 | 23,096 |
| Annual % Increase (69%) | 5% | 4% | 4% | 4% |
| Parsonage (0%) | 0 | 0 | 0 | 0 |
| Housing (2%) | 34,400 | 17,580 | 0 | 9,600 |
| Retirement (32%) | 1,457 | 1,768 | 1,627 | 1,788 |
| Life Insurance (29%) | 206 | 489 | 319 | 223 |
| Health Insurance (50%) | 3,1942 | 2,788 | 2,563 | 3,002 |
| Vacation/weeks (92%) | 2 | 3 | 3 | 3 |
| Education Funds (14%) | 670 | 331 | 250 | 342 |
| Auto Allowance (66%) | 66% | 63% | 78% | 72% |

* The percentage following each compensation item indicates the portion of all church bookkeepers who received that form of compensation. The averages in each column are for those individuals who actually received that compensation item. Auto allowance is included as part of base salary. See Chapter 3 for a full explanation of how to read this table.

### Total Compensation Comparisons

| Years Employed | 0-5 | 6-10 | 11-15 | over 15 |
|---|---|---|---|---|
| Average attendance | 996 | 972 | 802 | 792 |
| Average church income | 1,543,769 | 1,517,457 | 1,274,303 | 1,293,598 |
| Average years employed | 2 | 8 | 13 | 22 |
| Average compensation* | 23,475 | 23,513 | 24,630 | 25,782 |
| Standard deviation | 7,702 | 8,127 | 8,824 | 6,658 |

National average for all bookkeepers: $23,839 with a standard deviation of $7,890 (see Chapter 4, Table 4-3)

Total respondents: 258

* includes base salary, housing or parsonage allowance, retirement contribution, life and health insurance payments, and educational funds (note: auto allowance is included in base salary).

### Table 11-8: Annual Compensation Of Part-Time Bookkeepers By Hours Worked

| Hours-per-week | 1-14 | 15-29 | 30-39 | All Part-time |
|---|---|---|---|---|
| Number Of Respondents | 38 | 66 | 23 | 329 |
| Salary(89%*) | 4,231 | 9,636 | 16,368 | 8,585 |
| Annual % Increase (52%) | 4 | 5 | 8 | 5 |
| Parsonage (0%) | 12,000 | 0 | 0 | 0 |
| Housing (1%) | 0 | 1,360 | 0 | 2,585 |
| Retirement (6%) | 5,500 | 636 | 1,349 | 1,213 |
| Life Insurance (3%) | 0 | 62 | 85 | 114 |
| Health Insurance (6%) | 8,000 | 1,962 | 1,645 | 2,490 |
| Vacation/weeks (37%) | 2 | 2 | 3 | 2 |
| Education Funds (7%) | 800 | 196 | 325 | 254 |
| Auto Allowance (45%) | 42 | 68 | 83 | 45 |

* The percentage following each compensation item indicates the portion of all part-time church bookkeepers who received that form of compensation. The averages in each column are for those individuals who actually received that compensation item. Auto allowance is included as part of base salary. See Chapter 3 for a full explanation of how to read this table.

### Total Compensation Comparisons

| Hours Worked Per Week | 1-14 | 15-29 | 30-39 | All Part-time |
|---|---|---|---|---|
| Average attendance | 340 | 541 | 663 | 480 |
| Average church income | 386,965 | 642,586 | 944,623 | 589,621 |
| Average years employed | 6 | 5 | 6 | 6 |
| Average hours per week | 8 | 20 | 31 | 19 |
| Average compensation | 5,028 | 9,642 | 16,855 | 8,814 |
| Average hourly compensation* | 12.09 | 9.27 | 10.46 | 8.92 |
| Average hourly salary | 10.17 | 9.26 | 10.15 | 8.69 |

Total respondents: 329

* includes base salary, housing or parsonage allowance, retirement contribution, life and health insurance payments, and educational funds (note: auto allowance is included in base salary).

** includes base salary and auto allowance only; see discussion on "rounding errors" in Chapter 3.

# Chapter 12

# *Church Secretaries*

## Employment Profile

The title of church secretary can encompass a number of clerical and administrative roles within the church office. Church secretaries are the second most common paid position on the church staff following pastors. Almost all are church employees with 99% being female. One percent served as ordained ministers, although almost all viewed their work as both a ministry and a job. The secretaries surveyed provided the following employment profile:

|  | Full-time | Part-time |
|---|---|---|
| ☐ Number of Respondents | 1,312 | 979 |
| ☐ Ordained | 1% | 0% |
| ☐ Average Years Employed | 7 | 5 |
| ☐ Male | 1% | 2% |
| ☐ Female | 99% | 98% |
| ☐ Self-employed | 1% | 2% |
| ☐ Church Employee | 99% | 98% |
| ☐ High School Diploma | 57% | 59% |
| ☐ Associate Degree | 15% | 14% |
| ☐ Bachelor Degree | 26% | 23% |
| ☐ Master Degree | 2% | 4% |
| ☐ Doctorate | 0% | 0% |

## Compensation Analysis

The analysis below is based upon the tables found later in this chapter. The tables present compensation data according to worship attendance, church income, combinations of size and setting, gender, education, and years employed for church secretaries who serve full-time. The final table provides data for part-time church secretaries based upon the number of hours worked. In this way, the church secretary's compensation can be viewed from a variety of useful perspectives. The total compensation amount found in a separate box at the bottom of each page was calculated by adding the base salary (including auto allowance), housing or parsonage amount, life and health insurance payments, retirement contribution, and educational funds.

## Key Points

✎ *Secretarial compensation was not dramatically affected by church size.* Compensation for church secretaries increased only gradually with size and increased most rapidly when church attendance reached 200 and 1,000. The national average compensation corresponded with a church size of about 500 people. Secretaries serving in smaller congregations were paid substantially less than the national average. *See Table 12-1.*

✎ *Church income had an impact on secretarial income.* Similar to attendance, total compensation increased only gradually with size. The national average compensation was obtained with church incomes around $550,000. The biggest increases occurred once church income passed the $300,000 mark and again as it approached $2,000,000. *See Table 12-2.*

✎ *Suburban and urban churches provided the best compensation for smaller churches.* These churches achieved the national average compensation with an attendance of under 300 people. Churches in other settings paid considerably less, although the fringe benefits were comparable. *See Table 12-3.*

✎ *Urban churches provided the best compensation for larger churches with an average attendance over 500.* All larger churches provided a compensation package near or above the national average. *See Table 12-4.*

✎ *Ninety-nine percent of these church secretaries were women.* The few men who participated in this study reported an annual compensation less than that of women. The male secretaries in this study tended to serve smaller congregations, and had worked less years than the female secretaries. *See Table 12-5.*

✎ *Educational attainment had little impact on compensation.* The true controlling factors were attendance and church income. Those secretaries with college degrees earned the most, although it is not clear that the higher income is attributable to education. *See Table 12-6.*

✎ *Years employed had some impact on compensation.* A secretary who had worked thirteen years earned about the same as one who had worked twenty years. Over half of these secretaries had worked on average only three years. About 9% had worked more than fifteen years. *See Table 12-7.*

✎ *Part-time secretaries earn less per hour than do their full-time counterparts.* The typical part-time church secretary works about three days per week. Some part-time secretaries do not receive a salary, but rather receive their compensation as fringe benefits. *See Table 12-8.*

# Benefit Analysis

**Full-time staff members.** Church secretaries received less benefits for full-time work than ministerial and professional staff. Housing allowances were negligible. Only 43% received health insurance, less than any other position surveyed in this study. Benefits levels for secretaries were on par with those received by church custodial workers.

**Part-time staff members.** Forty-three percent of church secretaries worked part-time. The largest percentage worked over 30 hours per week. Ninety-eight percent of church secretaries working part-time were employees of the church and 2% were self-employed. Few benefits were provided for part-time church secretaries apart from paid vacation.

| Benefits | Full-time | Part-time |
| --- | --- | --- |
| ☐ Housing allowance | 0% | 0% |
| ☐ Parsonage provided | 0% | 0% |
| ☐ Retirement | 26% | 5% |
| ☐ Life insurance | 18% | 2% |
| ☐ Health insurance | 43% | 6% |
| ☐ Paid vacation | 89% | 49% |
| ☐ Auto allowance | 14% | 1% |
| ☐ Continuing education funds | 14% | 8% |

# Five Year Compensation Trend: National Averages for Church Secretaries

| | |
| --- | --- |
| ☐ 1993 | $17,442 |
| ☐ 1994 | $18,595 |
| ☐ 1995 | $18,858 |
| ☐ 1996 | $19,178 |
| ☐ 1997 | $20,232 |

## Table 12-1: Annual Compensation Of Secretary By Worship Attendance

| Church Attendance | 0-99 | 100-299 | 300-499 | 500-749 | 750-999 | over 1,000 |
|---|---|---|---|---|---|---|
| Number Of Respondents | 17 | 412 | 339 | 216 | 114 | 184 |
| Salary (97%*) | 17,527 | 17,308 | 18,607 | 19,309 | 20,993 | 22,197 |
| Annual % Increase (67%) | 5% | 5% | 5% | 5% | 4% | 4% |
| Parsonage (0%) | 0 | 0 | 0 | 0 | 0 | 0 |
| Housing (0%) | 0 | 0 | 0 | 0 | 0 | 0 |
| Retirement (26%) | 1,402 | 1,552 | 1,501 | 1,363 | 1,386 | 1,412 |
| Life Insurance (18%) | 0 | 856 | 265 | 312 | 248 | 770 |
| Health Insurance (43%) | 1,913 | 2,165 | 2,542 | 2,849 | 2,668 | 3,109 |
| Vacation/weeks (89%) | 3 | 3 | 2 | 2 | 3 | 3 |
| Education Funds (14%) | 167 | 292 | 335 | 330 | 474 | 333 |
| Receive Auto Allow. (14%) | 0% | 21% | 19% | 37% | 48% | 52% |

* The percentage following each compensation item indicates the portion of church secretaries who received that form of compensation. The averages in each column are for those individuals who actually received that compensation item. Auto allowance is included as part of base salary. See Chapter 3 for a full explanation of how to read this table.

## Total Compensation Comparisons

| Church Attendance | 0-99 | 100-299 | 300-499 | 500-749 | 750-999 | over 1,000 |
|---|---|---|---|---|---|---|
| Average attendance | 64 | 200 | 374 | 584 | 848 | 1,736 |
| Average church income | 191,780 | 275,830 | 477,069 | 795,183 | 1,124,257 | 2,082,812 |
| Average years employed | 12 | 7 | 7 | 7 | 7 | 8 |
| Average compensation* | 18,594 | 18,308 | 19,565 | 20,778 | 22,192 | 23,712 |
| Standard deviation | 7,939 | 5,750 | 5,933 | 5,881 | 6,081 | 6,941 |

National average for all secretaries: $20,232 with a standard deviation of $6,467 (see Chapter 4, Table 4-3).

Total respondents: 1,282

* includes base salary, housing or parsonage allowance, retirement contribution, life and health insurance payments, and educational funds (note: auto allowance is included in base salary).

## Table 12-2: Annual Compensation Of Secretary By Church Income

| Church Income in $ | 0-249,999 | 250,000-499,999 | 500,000-749,000 | 750,000-999,999 | 1,000,000 + |
|---|---|---|---|---|---|
| Number Of Respondents | 217 | 348 | 172 | 92 | 267 |
| Salary (97%*) | 16,050 | 18,293 | 19,982 | 19,591 | 21,926 |
| Annual % Increase (67%) | 5% | 5% | 4% | 4% | 4% |
| Parsonage (0%) | 0 | 0 | 0 | 0 | 0 |
| Housing (0%) | 0 | 0 | 0 | 0 | 0 |
| Retirement (26%) | 1,578 | 1,448 | 1,411 | 1,376 | 1,459 |
| Life Insurance (18%) | 207 | 685 | 342 | 505 | 591 |
| Health Insurance (43%) | 2,225 | 2,448 | 2,330 | 2,830 | 3,206 |
| Vacation/weeks (89%) | 2 | 3 | 2 | 2 | 3 |
| Education Funds (14%) | 249 | 321 | 330 | 391 | 411 |
| Receive Auto Allow. (14%) | 15% | 25% | 35% | 43% | 59% |

* The percentage following each compensation item indicates the portion of church secretaries who received that form of compensation. The averages in each column are for those individuals who actually received that compensation item. Auto allowance is included as part of base salary. See Chapter 3 for a full explanation of how to read this table.

## Total Compensation Comparisons

| Church Budget | 0-249,999 | 250,000-499,999 | 500,000-749,999 | 750,000-999,999 | 1,000,000+ |
|---|---|---|---|---|---|
| Average attendance | 209 | 324 | 498 | 703 | 1,294 |
| Average church income | 174,837 | 346,159 | 592,695 | 849,639 | 1,858,710 |
| Average years employed | 7 | 7 | 6 | 6 | 8 |
| Average compensation* | 17,019 | 19,559 | 21,356 | 20,395 | 23,626 |
| Standard deviation | 5,175 | 5,107 | 5,720 | 6,852 | 6,651 |

National average for all secretaries: $20,232 with a standard deviation of $6,467 (see Chapter 4, Table 4-3).

Total respondents: 1,096

* includes base salary, housing or parsonage allowance, retirement contribution, life and health insurance payments, and educational funds (note: auto allowance is included in base salary).

## Table 12-3: Annual Compensation Of Secretary By Church Setting And Size

| Attendance Under 500 | Urban | Suburban | Medium City | Small Town | Rural |
|---|---|---|---|---|---|
| Number Of Respondents | 103 | 213 | 203 | 197 | 39 |
| Salary (97%*) | 19,659 | 19,269 | 17,456 | 16,381 | 15,771 |
| Annual % Increase (67%) | 4% | 5% | 5% | 4% | 4% |
| Parsonage (0%) | 0 | 0 | 0 | 0 | 0 |
| Housing (0%) | 0 | 0 | 0 | 0 | 0 |
| Retirement (26%) | 1,900 | 1,482 | 1,470 | 1,383 | 1,558 |
| Life Insurance (18%) | 1,253 | 786 | 197 | 197 | 328 |
| Health Insurance (43%) | 2,207 | 2,839 | 2,120 | 2,058 | 2,533 |
| Vacation/weeks (89%) | 2 | 3 | 2 | 2 | 2 |
| Education Funds (14%) | 292 | 338 | 316 | 298 | 302 |
| Receive Auto Allow. (14%) | 19% | 29% | 19% | 23% | 13% |

* The percentage following each compensation item indicates the portion of church secretaries who received that form of compensation. The averages in each column are for those individuals who actually received that compensation item. Auto allowance is included as part of base salary. See Chapter 3 for a full explanation of how to read this table.

## Total Compensation Comparisons

| Attendance Under 500 | Urban | Suburban | Medium City | Small Town | Rural |
|---|---|---|---|---|---|
| Average attendance | 254 | 294 | 280 | 259 | 253 |
| Average church income | 424,578 | 425,043 | 338,491 | 304,330 | 261,963 |
| Average years employed | 7 | 7 | 7 | 7 | 8 |
| Average compensation* | 20,910 | 20,428 | 18,545 | 17,068 | 16,044 |
| Standard deviation | 7,169 | 6,295 | 4,949 | 4,890 | 5,560 |

National average for all secretaries: $20,232 with a standard deviation of $6,467 (see Chapter 4, Table 4-3).

Total respondents: 1,071

* includes base salary, housing or parsonage allowance, retirement contribution, life and health insurance payments, and educational funds (note: auto allowance is included in base salary).

## Table 12-4: Annual Compensation Of Secretary By Church Setting And Size

| Attendance Over 499 | Urban | Suburban | Medium City | Small Town | Rural |
|---|---|---|---|---|---|
| Number Of Respondents | 67 | 220 | 152 | 64 | 5 |
| Salary (97%*) | 21,581 | 21,995 | 19,302 | 18,687 | 18,870 |
| Annual % Increase (67%) | 5% | 5% | 4% | 4% | 8% |
| Parsonage (0%) | 0 | 0 | 0 | 0 | 0 |
| Housing (0%) | 0 | 0 | 0 | 0 | 0 |
| Retirement (26%) | 1,562 | 1,427 | 1,337 | 1,096 | 1,650 |
| Life Insurance (18%) | 268 | 521 | 771 | 137 | 0 |
| Health Insurance (43%) | 3,377 | 2,857 | 2,791 | 2,896 | 2,132 |
| Vacation/weeks (89%) | 2 | 3 | 3 | 3 | 2 |
| Education Funds (14%) | 511 | 390 | 213 | 347 | 300 |
| Receive Auto Allow. (14%) | 48% | 49% | 41% | 41% | 40% |

* The percentage following each compensation item indicates the portion of church secretaries who received that form of compensation. The averages in each column are for those individuals who actually received that compensation item. Auto allowance is included as part of base salary. See Chapter 3 for a full explanation of how to read this table.

## Total Compensation Comparisons

| Attendance Over 499 | Urban | Suburban | Medium City | Small Town | Rural |
|---|---|---|---|---|---|
| Average attendance | 977 | 1,218 | 942 | 867 | 950 |
| Average church income | 1,356,621 | 1,610,307 | 1,122,234 | 985,317 | 807,800 |
| Average years employed | 7 | 7 | 7 | 7 | 2 |
| Average compensation* | 23,605 | 23,147 | 20,915 | 20,112 | 19,686 |
| Standard deviation | 6,615 | 7,195 | 5,102 | 5,736 | 2,693 |

National average for all secretaries: $20,232 with a standard deviation of $6,467 (see Chapter 4, Table 4-3).

Total respondents: 508

* includes base salary, housing or parsonage allowance, retirement contribution, life and health insurance payments, and educational funds (note: auto allowance is included in base salary).

## Table 12-5: Annual Compensation Of Secretary By Gender

| Gender | Male | Female |
|---|---|---|
| Number Of Respondents | 12 | 1,277 |
| Salary (97%*) | 16,530 | 19,064 |
| Annual % Increase (67%) | 4% | 5% |
| Parsonage (0%) | 0 | 0 |
| Housing (0%) | 0 | 0 |
| Retirement (26%) | 2,000 | 1,481 |
| Life Insurance (18%) | 156 | 530 |
| Health Insurance (43%) | 2,227 | 2,640 |
| Vacation/weeks (89%) | 2 | 3 |
| Education Funds (14%) | 150 | 330 |
| Receive Auto Allow. (14%) | 42% | 32% |

* The percentage following each compensation item indicates the portion of church secretaries who received that form of compensation. The averages in each column are for those individuals who actually received that compensation item. Auto allowance is included as part of base salary. See Chapter 3 for a full explanation of how to read this table.

## Total Compensation Comparisons

| Gender | Male | Female |
|---|---|---|
| Average attendance | 235 | 591 |
| Average church income | 376,364 | 768,991 |
| Average years employed | 4 | 7 |
| Average compensation* | 19,170 | 20,282 |
| Standard deviation | 7,831 | 6,369 |

National average for all secretaries: $20,232 with a standard deviation of $6,467 (see Chapter 4, Table 4-3).

Total respondents: 1,289

* includes base salary, housing or parsonage allowance, retirement contribution, life and health insurance payments, and educational funds (note: auto allowance is included in base salary).

## Table 12-6: Annual Compensation Of Secretary By Education

| Highest Degree | High School | Associate | Bachelor | Master | Doctorate |
|---|---|---|---|---|---|
| Number Of Respondents | 529 | 197 | 243 | 22 | 0 |
| Salary (97%*) | 18,726 | 18,643 | 19,974 | 19,234 | |
| Annual % Increase (67%) | 4% | 4% | 5% | 4% | |
| Parsonage (0%) | 0 | 0 | 0 | 0 | |
| Housing (0%) | 0 | 0 | 0 | 0 | |
| Retirement (26%) | 1,410 | 1,576 | 1,507 | 1,790 | |
| Life Insurance (18%) | 672 | 715 | 509 | 174 | |
| Health Insurance (43%) | 2,698 | 2,697 | 2,475 | 2,628 | |
| Vacation/weeks (89%) | 3 | 3 | 2 | 2 | |
| Education Funds (14%) | 365 | 232 | 304 | 260 | |
| Receive Auto Allow. (14%) | 30% | 16% | 31% | 23% | |

* The percentage following each compensation item indicates the portion of church secretaries who received that form of compensation. The averages in each column are for those individuals who actually received that compensation item. Auto allowance is included as part of base salary. See Chapter 3 for a full explanation of how to read this table.

## Total Compensation Comparisons

| Highest Degree | High School | Associate | Bachelor | Master | Doctorate |
|---|---|---|---|---|---|
| Average attendance | 587 | 465 | 607 | 439 | |
| Average church income | 743,064 | 573,579 | 849,924 | 518,964 | |
| Average years employed | 7 | 7 | 6 | 5 | |
| Average compensation | 19,864 | 19,771 | 21,395 | 20,598 | |
| Standard deviation | 6,149 | 6,464 | 6,981 | 4,500 | |

National average for all secretaries: $20,232 with a standard deviation of $6,467 (see Chapter 4, Table 4-3).

Total respondents: 991

* includes base salary, housing or parsonage allowance, retirement contribution, life and health insurance payments, and educational funds (note: auto allowance is included in base salary).

## Table 12-7: Annual Compensation Of Secretary By Years Employed

| Years Employed | 0-5 | 6-10 | 11-15 | over 15 |
|---|---|---|---|---|
| Number Of Respondents | 661 | 323 | 170 | 120 |
| Salary (97%*) | 18,310 | 19,475 | 20,172 | 20,088 |
| Annual % Increase (67%) | 5% | 4% | 4% | 4% |
| Parsonage (0%) | 0 | 0 | 0 | 0 |
| Housing (0%) | 0 | 0 | 0 | 0 |
| Retirement (26%) | 1,506 | 1,226 | 1,402 | 2,048 |
| Life Insurance (18%) | 517 | 676 | 643 | 224 |
| Health Insurance (43%) | 2,421 | 2,532 | 3,075 | 3,102 |
| Vacation/weeks (89%) | 2 | 3 | 3 | 4 |
| Education Funds (14%) | 349 | 269 | 312 | 429 |
| Receive Auto Allow. (14%) | 32% | 32% | 31% | 33% |

\* The percentage following each compensation item indicates the portion of church secretaries who received that form of compensation. The averages in each column are for those individuals who actually received that compensation item. Auto allowance is included as part of base salary. See Chapter 3 for a full explanation of how to read this table.

## Total Compensation Comparisons

| Years Employed | 0-5 | 6-10 | 11-15 | over 15 |
|---|---|---|---|---|
| Average attendance | 550 | 621 | 651 | 631 |
| Average church income | 707,054 | 796,667 | 821,084 | 899,653 |
| Average years employed | 3 | 8 | 13 | 20 |
| Average compensation* | 19,296 | 20,708 | 21,725 | 21,989 |
| Standard deviation | 6,118 | 5,879 | 6,390 | 7,364 |

National average for all secretaries: $20,232 with a standard deviation of $6,467 (see Chapter 4, Table 4-3).

Total respondents: 1,274

\* includes base salary, housing or parsonage allowance, retirement contribution, life and health insurance payments, and educational funds (note: auto allowance is included in base salary).

## Table 12-8: Annual Compensation Of Part-Time Secretaries By Hours Worked

| Hours-per-week | under 15 | 15-29 | 30-39 | All Part-time |
|---|---|---|---|---|
| Number Of Respondents | 44 | 422 | 506 | 979** |
| Salary (91%*) | 6,692 | 9,219 | 15,615 | 12,424 |
| Annual % Increase (53%) | 5% | 5% | 4% | 4% |
| Parsonage (0%) | 0 | 0 | 0 | 0 |
| Housing (0%) | 0 | 0 | 0 | 0 |
| Retirement (5%) | 1,016 | 760 | 1,462 | 1,315 |
| Life Insurance (2%) | 0 | 0 | 555 | 539 |
| Health Insurance (6%) | 3,084 | 2,123 | 2,249 | 2,255 |
| Vacation/weeks (49%) | 2 | 2 | 3 | 2 |
| Education Funds (8%) | 200 | 177 | 279 | 251 |
| Receive Auto Allow. (1%) | 0% | 0% | 1% | 0% |

* The percentage following each compensation item indicates the portion of part-time church secretaries who received that form of compensation. The averages in each column are for those individuals who actually received that compensation item. Auto allowance is included as part of base salary. See Chapter 3 for a full explanation of how to read this table.

** Some respondents did not indicate the number of hours worked.

## Total Compensation Comparisons

| Hours Worked Per Week | under 15 | 15-29 | 30-39 | All Part-time |
|---|---|---|---|---|
| Average attendance | 120 | 229 | 339 | 280 |
| Average church income | 124,326 | 228,108 | 347,217 | 286,304 |
| Average years employed | 7 | 6 | 7 | 7 |
| Average hours per week | 11 | 22 | 33 | 27 |
| Average compensation | 6,989 | 9,322 | 16,220 | 12,808 |
| Ave. hourly compensation* | 12.22 | 8.15 | 9.45 | 9.12 |
| Average hourly salary** | 11.70 | 8.06 | 9.10 | 8.85 |

Total respondents: 979

* includes base salary, housing or parsonage allowance, retirement contribution, life and health insurance payments, and educational funds (note: auto allowance is included in base salary).

** includes base salary and auto allowance only; see discussion on "rounding errors" in Chapter 3.

# Chapter 13

# *Church Custodians*

## Employment profile

Church custodians normally receive an hourly wage and function as church employees. Most are men, although women represent 43% of those working part-time. Some custodians are ordained ministers. The custodians surveyed provided the following employment profile:

| Respondents: | Full-time | Part-time |
|---|---|---|
| ☐ Number of Respondents | 484 | 584 |
| ☐ Ordained | 2% | 1% |
| ☐ Average Years Employed | 6 | 5 |
| ☐ Male | 86% | 57% |
| ☐ Female | 14% | 43% |
| ☐ Self-employed | 1% | 13% |
| ☐ Church Employee | 99% | 87% |
| ☐ High School Diploma | 84% | 85% |
| ☐ Associate's Degree | 5% | 3% |
| ☐ Bachelor's Degree | 10% | 10% |
| ☐ Master's Degree | 1% | 2% |
| ☐ Doctorate | 0% | 0% |

## Compensation Analysis

The analysis below is based upon the tables found later in this chapter. The tables present compensation data according to worship attendance, church income, combinations of size and setting, gender, education, and years employed for church custodians who serve full-time. The final table provides data for part-time church custodians based upon the number of hours worked. In this way, the church custodian's compensation can be viewed from a variety of useful perspectives. For part-time workers, the average hourly compensation includes the base salary (including housing allowance), housing or parsonage amount, life and health insurance payments, retirement contribution, and educational funds.

## Key Points

✎ *Compensation increased gradually with church size.* The national average compensation corresponded to a church size of over 500 people. *See Table 13-1.*

✎ *The church's income was more of a predictor of compensation than was church size.* Compensation increased steadily with church income. The highest compensation levels occurred when churches had incomes over $2,000,000. *See Table 13-2.*

✎ *Suburban churches provided the best income for churches with an average attendance below 500.* This income was close to, but still below the national average. *See Table 13-3.*

✎ *Urban and Suburban churches provided the best income for churches with an average attendance above 500.* All congregations with an attendance above 500 provided compensation levels above or near the national average. *See Table 13-4.*

✎ *A significant difference existed in compensation levels between men and women.* In general, men earned almost $6,600 per year more than did women. Yet, on average, the women in this study worked more years than did their male counterparts. Males worked in slightly larger congregations, with larger budgets than the congregations in which the female custodians served. *See Table 13-5.*

✎ **Most custodians are high school graduates.** About 7% were college graduates. In general, compensation did increase for those with higher education. Individuals with college degrees earned about 17% more than those with a high school diploma. *See Table 13-6.*

✎ *Compensation increased with years served.* Those serving over 15 years earned the most. Those with five or less years of service earned below the national average. *See Table 13-7.*

✎ *On an hourly basis, part-time custodians earn less per hour than their full-time counterparts.* Most part-time custodians work about 16 hours per week. *See Table 13-8.*

# Benefit Analysis

**Full-time staff members.** Church custodians received fewer and smaller benefits than full-time ministerial or professional staff. About half received health insurance, but less than one-third had any retirement program from the church. Benefits received were less than bookkeepers and more than secretaries.

**Part-time church staff.** More church custodians worked part-time than full-time. Fifty-five percent were part-time employees. Of this group, 43% were women. Thirteen percent of the part-time custodians were self-employed. Churches provided part-time custodial workers very few benefits as compared to full-time employees. Apart from benefits such as a paid vacation, part-time custodial work is primarily a straight hourly wage position.

| Benefits | Full-time | Part-time |
|---|---|---|
| ❏ Housing allowance | 1% | 0% |
| ❏ Parsonage provided | 1% | 0% |
| ❏ Retirement | 27% | 2% |
| ❏ Life insurance | 22% | 1% |
| ❏ Health insurance | 52% | 4% |
| ❏ Paid vacation | 88% | 30% |
| ❏ Auto allowance | 62% | 35% |
| ❏ Continuing educational funds | 4% | 1% |

# Five Year Compensation Trend: National Averages for Church Custodians

| | | |
|---|---|---|
| ❏ | 1993 | $18,617 |
| ❏ | 1994 | $20,541 |
| ❏ | 1995 | $20,161 |
| ❏ | 1996 | $21,608 |
| ❏ | 1997 | $22,493 |

## Table 13-1: Annual Compensation Of Custodian By Worship Attendance

| Church Attendance | 0-99 | 100-299 | 300-499 | 500-749 | 750-999 | over 1,000 |
|---|---|---|---|---|---|---|
| Number | 0 | 76 | 100 | 108 | 67 | 115 |
| Salary (96%*) | | 15,502 | 19,511 | 20,625 | 21,598 | 23,333 |
| Annual % Increase (63%) | | 4% | 4% | 4% | 4% | 4% |
| Parsonage (1%) | | 12,000 | 0 | 10,200 | 0 | 0 |
| Housing (1%) | | 6,600 | 13,640 | 0 | 18,540 | 9,050 |
| Retirement (27%) | | 1,864 | 1,857 | 1,341 | 1,629 | 1,354 |
| Life Insurance (22%) | | 890 | 224 | 379 | 151 | 310 |
| Health Insurance (52%) | | 3,493 | 3,027 | 3,026 | 3,057 | 3,711 |
| Vacation/weeks (88%) | | 2 | 2 | 2 | 2 | 2 |
| Education Funds (4%) | | 1,000 | 157 | 233 | 433 | 390 |
| Receive Auto Allow. (60%) | | 33% | 50% | 66% | 66% | 78% |

* The percentage following each compensation item indicate the portion of church custodians who received that form of compensation. The averages in each column are for those individuals who actually received that compensation item. Auto allowance is included as part of base salary. See Chapter 3 for a full explanation of how to read this table.

## Total Compensation Comparisons At A Glance

| Worship Attendance | 0-99 | 100-299 | 300-499 | 500-749 | 750-999 | over 1,000 |
|---|---|---|---|---|---|---|
| Average attendance | | 204 | 383 | 597 | 848 | 1,794 |
| Average church income | | 328,822 | 584,312 | 914,850 | 1,294,224 | 2,088,241 |
| Average years employed | | 6 | 7 | 7 | 6 | 7 |
| Average compensation* | | 17,114 | 21,049 | 22,809 | 23,525 | 26,251 |
| Standard deviation | | 8,228 | 8,952 | 8,379 | 7,475 | 8,176 |

National average for all custodians: $22,493 with a standard deviation of $8,983 (see Chapter 4, Table 4-3)

Total respondents: 466

* includes base salary, housing or parsonage allowance, retirement contributions, life and health insurance payments, and educational funds (note:auto allowance is included in base salary).

## Table 13-2: Annual Compensation Of Custodian By Church Budget

| Church Budget in $ | 0-249,999 | 250,000-499,999 | 500,000-749,000 | 750,000-999,999 | 1,000,000 + |
|---|---|---|---|---|---|
| Number Of Respondents | 31 | 84 | 90 | 50 | 187 |
| Salary (96%*) | 14,250 | 16,117 | 19,918 | 20,690 | 23,212 |
| Annual % Increase (63%) | 4% | 4% | 4% | 4% | 4% |
| Parsonage (1%) | 0 | 12,000 | 12,000 | 0 | 6,201 |
| Housing (1%) | 0 | 8,100 | 0 | 18,110 | 9,050 |
| Retirement (27%) | 1,260 | 1,678 | 1,482 | 1,419 | 1,501 |
| Life Insurance (22%) | 300 | 862 | 394 | 641 | 203 |
| Health Insurance (52%) | 2,994 | 2,951 | 3,270 | 2,908 | 3,574 |
| Vacation/weeks (88%) | 2 | 2 | 2 | 2 | 3 |
| Education Funds (4%) | 0 | 488 | 121 | 75 | 385 |
| Receive Auto Allow. (60%) | 35% | 36% | 52% | 6%0 | 76% |

\* The percentage following each compensation item indicate the portion of church custodians who received that form of compensation. The averages in each column are for those individuals who actually received that compensation item. Auto allowance is included as part of base salary. See Chapter 3 for a full explanation of how to read this table.

## Total Compensation Comparisons

| Church Budget | 0-249,000 | 250,000-499,999 | 500,000-749,999 | 750,000-999,999 | 1,000,000+ |
|---|---|---|---|---|---|
| Average attendance | 244 | 341 | 491 | 690 | 1,354 |
| Average church income | 1,756,686 | 361,248 | 604,653 | 853,262 | 1,897,686 |
| Average years employed | 4 | 6 | 6 | 7 | 7 |
| Average compensation* | 15,170 | 17,549 | 21,862 | 22,160 | 26,094 |
| Standard deviation | 6,027 | 7,879 | 8,230 | 7,262 | 8,738 |

National average for all custodians: $22,493 with a standard deviation of $8,983 (see Chapter 4, Table 4-3)

Total respondents: 442

\* includes base salary, housing or parsonage allowance, retirement contributions, life and health insurance payments, and educational funds (note:auto allowance is included in base salary).

## Table 13-3: Annual Compensation Of Custodian By Church Setting And Size

| Attendance Under 500 | Urban | Suburban | Medium City | Small Town | Rural |
|---|---|---|---|---|---|
| Number Of Respondents | 18 | 55 | 59 | 41 | 2 |
| Salary (96%*) | 19,558 | 19,730 | 17,716 | 15,212 | 10,900 |
| Annual % Increase (63%) | 4% | 4% | 4% | 4% | 6% |
| Parsonage (1%) | 0 | 12,000 | 0 | 0 | 0 |
| Housing (1%) | 0 | 12,140 | 9,600 | 0 | 0 |
| Retirement (27%) | 1,271 | 2,249 | 1,810 | 1,348 | 0 |
| Life Insurance (22%) | 1,281 | 320 | 261 | 121 | 0 |
| Health Insurance (52%) | 2,692 | 3,599 | 3,279 | 2,502 | 0 |
| Vacation/weeks (88%) | 3 | 2 | 2 | 2 | 2 |
| Education Funds (4%) | 0 | 200 | 395 | 0 | 0 |
| Receive Auto Allow. (60%) | 50% | 58% | 39% | 78% | 0% |

* The percentage following each compensation item indicate the portion of church custodians who received that form of compensation. The averages in each column are for those individuals who actually received that compensation item. Auto allowance is included as part of base salary. See Chapter 3 for a full explanation of how to read this table.

## Total Compensation Comparisons

| Attendance Under 500 | Urban | Suburban | Medium City | Small Town | Rural |
|---|---|---|---|---|---|
| Average attendance | 320 | 311 | 316 | 280 | 188 |
| Average church income | 558,830 | 557,369 | 413,791 | 378,875 | 227,500 |
| Average years employed | 9 | 6 | 6 | 5 | 1 |
| Average compensation* | 21,770 | 22,003 | 18,855 | 16,077 | 10,900 |
| Standard deviation | 8,818 | 9,606 | 8,764 | 6,126 | 4,384 |

National average for all custodians: $22,493 with a standard deviation of $8,983 (see Chapter 4, Table 4-3)

Total respondents: 175

* includes base salary, housing or parsonage allowance, retirement contributions, life and health insurance payments, and educational funds (note:auto allowance is included in base salary).

## Table 13-4: Annual Compensation Of Custodian By Church Setting And Size

| Attendance Over 499 | Urban | Suburban | Medium City | Small Town | Rural |
|---|---|---|---|---|---|
| Number Of Respondents | 41 | 127 | 83 | 33 | 3 |
| Salary (96%*) | 22,301 | 22,929 | 20,926 | 20,576 | 16,022 |
| Annual % Increase (63%) | 5% | 4% | 4% | 4% | 0% |
| Parsonage (1%) | 4,200 | 7,202 | 12,000 | 0 | 0 |
| Housing (1%) | 8,500 | 9,600 | 18,540 | 0 | 0 |
| Retirement (27%) | 1,474 | 1,471 | 1,233 | 1,243 | 2,165 |
| Life Insurance (22%) | 104 | 347 | 383 | 201 | 200 |
| Health Insurance (52%) | 3,251 | 3,476 | 2,915 | 3,642 | 4,604 |
| Vacation/weeks (88%) | 3 | 3 | 2 | 2 | 2 |
| Education Funds (4%) | 360 | 2,832 | 300 | 550 | 300 |
| Receive Auto Allow. (60%) | 76% | 72% | 65% | 70% | 100% |

* The percentage following each compensation item indicate the portion of church custodians who received that form of compensation. The averages in each column are for those individuals who actually received that compensation item. Auto allowance is included as part of base salary. See Chapter 3 for a full explanation of how to read this table.

## Total Compensation Comparisons

| Attendance Over 499 | Urban | Suburban | Medium City | Small Town | Rural |
|---|---|---|---|---|---|
| Average attendance | 914 | 1,411 | 961 | 786 | 967 |
| Average church income | 1,547,251 | 1,754,426 | 1,234,368 | 1,029,664 | 1,019,667 |
| Average years employed | 7 | 6 | 6 | 7 | 11 |
| Average compensation* | 25,516 | 25,145 | 23,041 | 23,143 | 21,514 |
| Standard deviation | 8,895 | 8,992 | 6,878 | 7,864 | 4,581 |

National average for all custodians: $22,493 with a standard deviation of $8,983 (see Chapter 4, Table 4-3)

Total respondents: 287

* includes base salary, housing or parsonage allowance, retirement contributions, life and health insurance payments, and educational funds (note:auto allowance is included in base salary).

## Table 13-5: Annual Compensation Of Custodian By Gender

| Gender | Male | Female |
|---|---|---|
| Number Of Respondents | 415 | 66 |
| Salary (96%*) | 21,112 | 16,110 |
| Annual % Increase (63%) | 4% | 4% |
| Parsonage (1%) | 8,521 | 0 |
| Housing 1(%) | 11,660 | 0 |
| Retirement (27%) | 1,604 | 1,289 |
| Life Insurance (22%) | 359 | 401 |
| Health Insurance (52%) | 3,366 | 2,367 |
| Vacation/weeks (88%) | 2 | 2 |
| Education Funds (4%) | 309 | 371 |
| Receive Auto Allow. (60%) | 62% | 47% |

\* The percentage following each compensation item indicate the portion of church custodians who received that form of compensation. The averages in each column are for those individuals who actually received that compensation item. Auto allowance is included as part of base salary. See Chapter 3 for a full explanation of how to read this table.

## Total Compensation Comparisons

| Gender | Male | Female |
|---|---|---|
| Average attendance | 834 | 733 |
| Average church income | 1,137,201 | 925,367 |
| Average years employed | 6 | 7 |
| Average compensation* | 23,433 | 16,815 |
| Standard deviation | 8,881 | 7,062 |

National average for all custodians: $22,493 with a standard deviation of $8,983 (see Chapter 4, Table 4-3)

Total respondents 481

\* includes base salary, housing or parsonage allowance, retirement contributions, life and health insurance payments, and educational funds (note:auto allowance is included in base salary).

## Table 13-6: Annual Compensation Of Custodian By Education

| Highest Degree | High School | Associate | Bachelor | Master | Doctorate |
|---|---|---|---|---|---|
| Number Of Respondents | 244 | 15 | 28 | 2 | 0 |
| Salary (96%*) | 20,425 | 18,941 | 22,754 | 19,308 | |
| Annual % Increase (63%) | 4% | 4% | 5% | 4% | |
| Parsonage (1%) | 9,400 | 0 | 0 | 0 | |
| Housing (1%) | 11,245 | 0 | 9,050 | 0 | |
| Retirement (27%) | 1,634 | 1,745 | 1,478 | 0 | |
| Life Insurance (22%) | 591 | 231 | 162 | 0 | |
| Health Insurance (52%) | 3,449 | 2,685 | 3,453 | 3,630 | |
| Vacation/weeks (88%) | 2 | 2 | 3 | 2 | |
| Education Funds (4%) | 225 | 0 | 700 | 0 | |
| Receive Auto Allow. (60%) | 61% | 73% | 61% | 100% | |

* The percentage following each compensation item indicate the portion of church custodians who received that form of compensation. The averages in each column are for those individuals who actually received that compensation item. Auto allowance is included as part of base salary. See Chapter 3 for a full explanation of how to read this table.

## Total Compensation Comparisons

| Highest Degree | High School | Associate | Bachelor | Master | Doctorate |
|---|---|---|---|---|---|
| Average attendance | 770 | 626 | 826 | 745 | |
| Average church income | 1,136,103 | 947,074 | 1,296,209 | 700,000 | |
| Average years employed | 7 | 7 | 6 | 4 | |
| Average compensation* | 22,535 | 22,307 | 26,339 | 22,554 | |
| Standard deviation | 9,140 | 7,296 | 10,546 | 2,283 | |

National average for all custodians: $22,493 with a standard deviation of $8,983 (see Chapter 4, Table 4-3)

Total respondents: 289

* includes base salary, housing or parsonage allowance, retirement contributions, life and health insurance payments, and educational funds (note:auto allowance is included in base salary).

## Table 13-7: Annual Compensation Of Custodian By Years Employed

| Years Employed | 0-5 | 6-10 | 11-15 | over 15 |
|---|---|---|---|---|
| Number Of Respondents | 254 | 113 | 57 | 30 |
| Salary (96%*) | 19,991 | 20,636 | 21,269 | 23,920 |
| Annual % Increase (63%) | 4% | 4% | 4% | 3% |
| Parsonage (1%) | 5,401 | 12,000 | 0 | 14,400 |
| Housing (1%) | 13,580 | 8,850 | 9,600 | 0 |
| Retirement (27%) | 1,389 | 1,875 | 1,474 | 1,912 |
| Life Insurance (22%) | 281 | 799 | 419 | 223 |
| Health Insurance (52%) | 3,239 | 3,589 | 3,061 | 3,622 |
| Vacation/weeks (88%) | 2 | 3 | 3 | 4 |
| Education Funds (4%) | 429 | 157 | 300 | 100 |
| Receive Auto Allow. (60%) | 58% | 59% | 60% | 80% |

* The percentage following each compensation item indicate the portion of church custodians who received that form of compensation. The averages in each column are for those individuals who actually received that compensation item. Auto allowance is included as part of base salary. See Chapter 3 for a full explanation of how to read this table.

## Total Compensation Comparisons

| Years Employed | 0-5 | 6-10 | 11-15 | over 15 |
|---|---|---|---|---|
| Average attendance | 756 | 860 | 719 | 973 |
| Average church income | 1,048,310 | 1,104,307 | 1,111,447 | 1,772,249 |
| Average years employed | 3 | 8 | 13 | 22 |
| Average compensation* | 21,879 | 22,495 | 24,017 | 28,308 |
| Standard deviation | 8,621 | 9,504 | 8,393 | 9,400 |

National average for all custodians: $22,493 with a standard deviation of $8,983 (see Chapter 4, Table 4-3)

Total respondents: 454

* includes base salary, housing or parsonage allowance, retirement contributions, life and health insurance payments, and educational funds (note:auto allowance is included in base salary).

## Table 13-8: Annual Compensation Of Part-Time Custodians By Hours Worked

| Hours-per-week | 1-14 | 15-29 | 30-39 | All Part-time |
|---|---|---|---|---|
| Number Of Respondents | 77 | 109 | 17 | 584 |
| Salary (93%*) | 3,885 | 8,567 | 13,031 | 7,079 |
| Annual % Increase (45%) | 6% | 5% | 4% | 5% |
| Parsonage (0%) | 0 | 0 | 0 | 10,200 |
| Housing (0%) | 0 | 0 | 0 | 0 |
| Retirement (2%) | 1,608 | 1,382 | 0 | 1,411 |
| Life Insurance (1%) | 315 | 166 | 204 | 433 |
| Health Insurance (4%) | 2,510 | 2,918 | 1,758 | 2,529 |
| Vacation/weeks (30%) | 2 | 2 | 2 | 2 |
| Education Funds (1%) | 0 | 312 | 100 | 331 |
| Receive Auto Allow. (35%) | 48% | 58% | 71% | 35% |

* The percentage following each compensation item indicate the portion of part-time church custodians who received that form of compensation. The averages in each column are for those individuals who actually received that compensation item. Auto allowance is included as part of base salary. See Chapter 3 for a full explanation of how to read this table.

## Total Compensation Comparisons

| Hours Worked Per Week | 1-14 | 15-29 | 30-39 | All Part-time |
|---|---|---|---|---|
| Average attendance | 205 | 304 | 508 | 271 |
| Average church income | 204,293 | 339,361 | 761,812 | 305,537 |
| Average years employed | 5 | 5 | 3 | 5 |
| Average hours per week | 7 | 20 | 31 | 16 |
| Average compensation | 3,927 | 8,727 | 13,696 | 7,215 |
| Ave. hourly compensation* | 10.79 | 8.39 | 8.50 | 8.67 |
| Average hourly salary** | 10.67 | 8.24 | 8.08 | 8.51 |

Total respondents: 584

* includes base salary, housing or parsonage allowance, retirement contributions, life and health insurance payments, and educational funds (note:auto allowance is included in base salary).

Includes base salary and auto allowance only; see discussion on "rounding errors" in Chapter 3.

# Chapter 14

# *Statistical Abstract of Participating Churches*

In addition to the individual compensation surveys, many of the participating churches also completed a congregational profile. That information is presented below. First, data is presented according to Sunday worship attendance. Five size categories are portrayed. Second, attendance and income trends are presented according to both church *size* and *setting*.

## Key Findings

☐ Congregations with an attendance between 751-1,000 experienced the highest per capita giving; churches with an attendance under 250 had the lowest.

☐ About 36% of churches provide additional salary to their ordained staff members to assist them with their social security payments. Of those churches that do help, 36% pay one-half of the social security tax while 33% pay all of it.

☐ Eighty-eight percent of the participating churches reimburse the professional expenses of their ordained employees.

☐ The majority of churches (94%) require a full accounting of professional expenses including date, purpose, location, and amount of expense before a reimbursement is made.

☐ Only 33% of pastors believe their church has an effective training program for church treasures. Church treasurers reflect an even lower view. Only 25% feel that their church provides adequate training.

☐ A majority of congregations, regardless of church size or geographical location, have experienced an increase in church attendance over the past three years. The largest congregations have experienced the most growth.

☐ Fifty percent of the participating churches reported that their income exceeded their expenses during the past year. This percentage has increased every year for five consecutive years.

## Congregational Profile By Church Worship Attendance

|  | All<br>n=1,109 | 0-250<br>n=479 | 251-500<br>n=289 | 501-750<br>n=127 | 751-1000<br>n=74 | over 1000<br>n=100 |
|---|---|---|---|---|---|---|
| Worship Attendance | 469 | 150 | 370 | 625 | 885 | 1,773 |
| Total income | $642,914 | $183,774 | $517,814 | $850,895 | $1,289,840 | $2,326,374 |
| Per capita: attendance | $1,371 | $1,225 | $1,399 | $1,361 | $1,457 | $1,312 |
| Number of Ordained Staff | 2 | 1 | 2 | 3 | 4 | 7 |
| Number of Nonordained Staff (full-time) | 5 | 2 | 3 | 5 | 8 | 14 |
| Contributes to social security payments of ordained staff | 36% | 32% | 40% | 41% | 35% | 38% |
| Pays all | 33% | 40% | 30% | 27% | 25% | 31% |
| Pays half | 36% | 37% | 35% | 42% | 29% | 37% |
| Reimburses professional expenses | 88% | 87% | 87% | 88% | 92% | 92% |
| Requires a full accounting including date, purpose, location and amount before reimbursing expenses | 94% | 92% | 94% | 95% | 97% | 99% |
| Has effective training program for new board members | 33% | 26% | 37% | 42% | 46% | 28% |
| Has effective training program for church treasurers | 34% | 25% | 36% | 44% | 45% | 51% |

# Attendance and Income Trends by Church Size

| Attendance Trend Over the Past Three Years | Decline | Stable | Increase |
|---|---|---|---|
| All Churches | 9% | 33% | 58% |
| 0-250 (479) | 10% | 39% | 51% |
| 251-500 (289) | 10% | 30% | 60% |
| 501-750 (127) | 6% | 33% | 61% |
| 751-1000 (74) | 5% | 33% | 62% |
| over 1000 (100) | 2% | 18% | 80% |

| Financial Status | Income below expenses | Income meets expenses | Income above expenses |
|---|---|---|---|
| All churches | 14% | 37% | 50% |
| 0-250 (479) | 18% | 40% | 42% |
| 251-500 (289) | 10% | 39% | 51% |
| 501-750 (127) | 13% | 33% | 54% |
| 751-1000 (74) | 8% | 27% | 65% |
| over 1000 (100) | 4% | 23% | 73% |

## Attendance and Income Trends by Geographical Setting

| Attendance Trend Over the Past Three Years | Decline | Stable | Increase |
|---|---|---|---|
| All Churches (1,109) | 9% | 33% | 58% |
| Urban (129) | 6% | 43% | 51% |
| Suburban (421) | 9% | 30% | 61% |
| Medium Size City (245) | 9% | 33% | 58% |
| Small Town (233) | 10% | 35% | 55% |
| Rural (64) | 5% | 31% | 64% |

| Financial Status | Income below expenses | Income meets expenses | Income above expenses |
|---|---|---|---|
| All churches (1,109) | 14% | 37% | 50% |
| Urban (129) | 17% | 35% | 47% |
| Suburban (421) | 13% | 38% | 49% |
| Medium Size City (245) | 11% | 35% | 54% |
| Small Town (233) | 14% | 40% | 46% |
| Rural (64) | 12% | 32% | 56% |

# Appendix 1

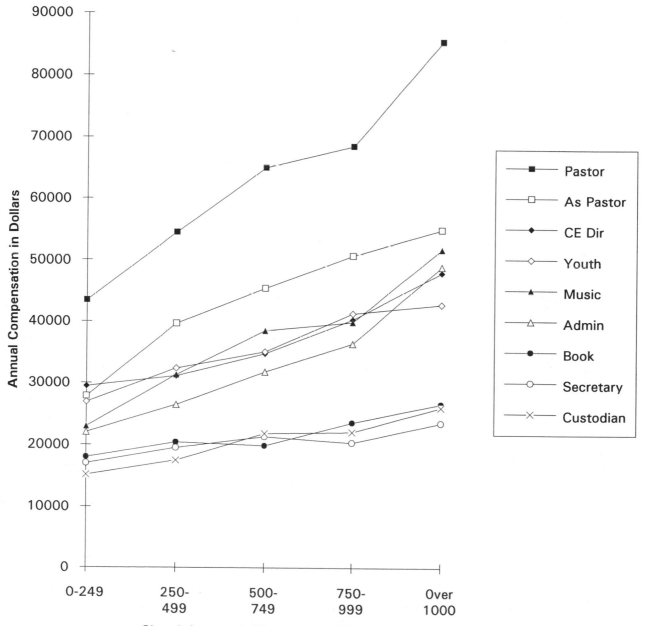

## Compensation and Church Income

Annual Compensation in Dollars

Church Income in Thousands of Dollars

Legend:
- Pastor
- As Pastor
- CE Dir
- Youth
- Music
- Admin
- Book
- Secretary
- Custodian

# Appendix 2

## *Five Year Compensation Trend*

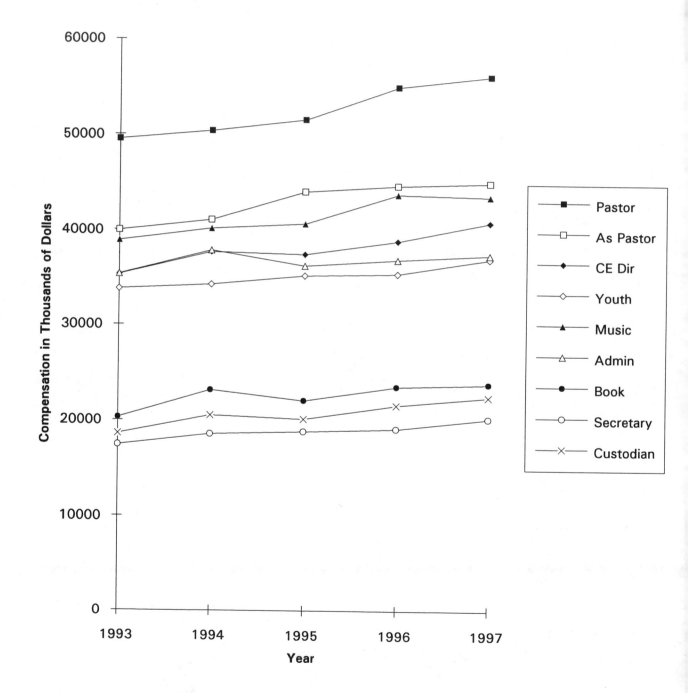